Introducing C

More books on computer languages

Introducing Logo
Boris Allan
0 246 12323 0

Introducing Pascal
Boris Allan
0 246 12322 2

micro-PROLOG and Artificial Intelligence
A. A. Berk
0 00 383158 2

LISP: The Language of Artificial Intelligence
A. A. Berk
0 00 383130 2

Exploring FORTH
Owen Bishop
0 246 12188 2

QL SuperBASIC
A. A. Berk
0 246 12596 9

Introducing C

Boris Allan

COLLINS
8 Grafton Street, London W1

Collins Professional and Technical Books
William Collins Sons & Co. Ltd
8 Grafton Street, London W1X 3LA

First published in Great Britain by
Collins Professional and Technical Books 1986

Distributed in the United States of America
by Sheridan House, Inc.

British Library Cataloguing in Publication Data
Allan, Boris
Introducing C.
1. C (Computer program language)
I. Title
005.2'6   QA76.73.C15

ISBN 0-00-383105-1

Typeset by V & M Graphics Ltd, Aylesbury, Bucks
Printed and bound in Great Britain by
Mackays of Chatham, Kent

Contents

Preface

In the writing of this book I have received assistance from various manufacturers and providers of C software. I would like to place on record my thanks for this assistance, and hasten to add that all mistakes are my responsibility.

The software providers, and their telephone numbers, are

Small-C-80	MMG Consultants, 06845 63555 (UK)
Microsoft C	Microsoft Corporation, 07535 59951 (UK),
Objective-C	Productivity Products International,
	(203) 426-1875 (USA)
	Unit-C, 0903 205233 (UK)
Instant-C	Rational Systems, Inc, (617) 653-6194 (USA)
Living C Personal	Living Software Ltd, 0272 217040 (UK),
	1800 (Toll free) 826-2612 (USA).

The Varith source (Appendix D) can be obtained in an MSDOS version for the price of the media and packaging. Those interested should write to me via my publishers for further details.

This book is dedicated to Maggie.

Chapter One
Why C?

C is probably the best applications and systems programming language generally available on small computers at present.

The key to C's success is that it works: C allows the programmer a control over the workings of the machine equalled only by a few other languages such as FORTH or Algol 68. If other languages can provide this control over the intimate workings of the machine, why has C become the *de facto* language for system development in many cases? The popularity of C has come about through the success of the language with programmers and system developers, and not through any commercial hype.

C is a language for programmers, and in particular programmers who have a good understanding of the workings of computers. C can be a language for those who wish to dabble in programming, without any particular interest in how a computer operates, but C is only used to advantage when the programmer is willing to take time to understand what is happening to the machine being used. On the west coast of the USA there is a tee-shirt slogan which says 'Real programmers don't write games', and on the back is the slogan 'If you C what I mean'.

The problem with other languages which allow such great control is that they tend to be either very large and expansive languages such as Algol 68, or idiosyncratic languages such as FORTH, which require special types of system to operate. C is not only a small compact language, but is also a language which produces standard compiled programs.

Compactness is important because (for example) Algol 68 cannot be successfully implemented on most microcomputers, whereas there are many versions of C. FORTH is not designed to produce standard compiled programs though there are versions of FORTH which can produce compiled stand alone programs (that is, programs which do not require the FORTH system to be present). The problems with using Algol 68 and FORTH for developing systems software on microcomputers are due principally to the fact that they were not developed explicitly for that purpose. C, however, was designed for the purpose of developing systems software – and it was well designed at that.

Some antecedents

C is a system programmer's language, where a system programmer writes software which not only performs a task but also provides an environment. C was developed as the language of UNIX, a very sophisticated and powerful operating system for minicomputers (which has been extended to mainframes and microcomputers), so C was developed as a language to produce systems. I give details of UNIX in Appendix B, but for now here are the salient points about UNIX which help to explain the success of C.

1. UNIX was written to produce an operating system for the person writing the system, and not as an operating system for some hypothetical customer. UNIX was written because Ken Thompson (its originator) wanted an operating system to help him in his work, thus the UNIX operating system was written for a practical purpose.
2. UNIX became a more comprehensive system by involving users; they were asked to contribute to the development of the environment – users in one installation were encouraged to share new applications with UNIX users in other installations. The sharing of software was via the medium of C, and this had certain principal effects on the form of the C programming language:

> 2.1. C had to be fairly standard across computers and installations, so that the source code for C was as compatible as can reasonably be expected of any computer language
> 2.2. Each type of computer, and each type of installation, has different physical characteristics, different configurations, different work patterns, and so C had to be able to provide facilities which were as machine independent as possible
> 2.3. As the contributed programs were to be part of a coherent whole, and there was a desire to reduce the duplication of effort, C had to have powerful (yet easy to use) methods of utilising existing software

3. UNIX was to be extensible and, as it was not an operating system which aimed to satisfy the lowest common denominator, the way in which UNIX communicated to the user was compact, powerful, and very expressive – one line of system instructions in UNIX can often encapsulate what would require special programs on some systems. As a consequence, the C programming language is itself compact, powerful, and very expressive.

The other very important influence on C is the language BCPL. The language C was directly developed from a language called B, which was directly developed from BCPL, and BCPL was itself directly developed from CPL, for it was Basic CPL. The meaning of CPL was the Common Programming Language, and CPL was directly developed ...

BCPL is discussed in Appendix A, but here are some salient points about the language:

1. BCPL was developed as a language to write compilers, that is, to produce a system to create systems.
2. It was designed to be simple and portable.
3. BCPL was characterised by a rich portfolio of methods for controlling execution, a far richer selection than was available with most other languages.
4. BCPL used only one data type, the bit pattern, which was the content of a memory location (a 'cell') expressed as a binary number.
5. BCPL was organised around a hypothetical computer, of which the most important characteristic was its 'store' – a linear arrangement of memory cells, where a variable in BCPL was no more than the name given to a memory cell.

That C has many of these characteristics explains its success, but C has made certain modifications to these aspects to enhance the language's ease of applicability. Possibly the most important change from BCPL to C is the expansion of the number of data types, but even so C allows the programmer to change the interpretation of data types if so desired (the C precursor, B, retained the notion of only one data type which came from BCPL).

Let us examine a complex system.

A complex system

This book was written using a word processor. Any word processor of power and flexibility is, in fact, a complex system; an environment in which one works to produce text documents. There are many word processors on the market, and I chose the one which suited me best. I wanted a word processor which suited my needs and desires, or at least one which could be modified to conform more closely to my needs and desires. I chose Perfect Writer II (PW II). I had already used the first version of Perfect Writer (PW), and the style of the system suited my style of work. PW in its original version was characterised by its capacity to be tailored to fit applications and peripheral devices; in fact, PW was a very programmable system. It is well worth considering the point that any system (such as a word processor, or a database, or a spreadsheet) is a new language to be learned, and what the software writer is producing when creating such a system is a new programming language. Any system which allows the user to control effects and produce novel results is a minor programming language.

The new version of the word processor, PW II, is more adaptable (and more programmable) than the old version, with extra facilities that increase its ease of use. The new version of the word processor is also upwardly compatible with the old version; anything I had written for the old version could be used for the new, but not all of my work using the new version was compatible with the old. PW II was thus designed to encompass the first version, but with enhancements to its ease of use and extensibility. How is this sophistication achieved?

The key to the successful adaptability of PW is the programming language C, in conjunction with the UNIX-like aim of promoting extensibility and adaptability. The original version of PW was written in C, and so is PW II, but what may appear rather surprising is that most other recent word processors are also written in C. The use of C in the production of software is not, however, merely restricted to word processors.

At present, most applications software is written in C or some variant of the language. Nearly all the large software houses in the USA and the UK program almost exclusively in C, and their software writers only drop down to machine code programming for extra speed in crucial aspects of an application. For example, I think that it is true to say that most newly implemented languages on microcomputers are initially written in C, including list processing languages such as LOGO (though at least one version of LOGO has been written in BCPL).

The structure of PW II has many similarities to any operating system, and thus the nature of PW II will benefit from some attention. As this is a book about C and not about Perfect software, the examination has to be cursory.

At one time, a word processor took the textual information typed in, perhaps modified the information in some way, and later sent the information to a printer. As printers changed and became more sophisticated, some of the early word processing programs merely had a different special installation program to cope with a new printer. The original version of Perfect Writer was one of the first of a new breed of word processor systems which were designed to be more adaptable, more extensible, and more 'intelligent', using ideas from modern operating systems such as UNIX.

For example, the same word processor on the same computer might be connected possibly to various printers, depending upon the application. The same word processor might be used on computer which at one time is connected to a daisywheel printer (for letter quality output), and half an hour later connected to a dot matrix printer for printing a long report. Later that day, the dot matrix printer might be used in a proportional output mode rather than in the standard mode.

The point is that the same word processor on the same computer can be called on to produce many different forms of output. To cope with such changes, therefore, a word processor can either have many different installation programs to set up the system, or have one installation program as part of the system which enables the user to change easily between types of output. A further complication is that the same document might be required in many different formats, for example, a single spaced condensed format for checking, and a double spaced daisywheel print format for the final document.

All these considerations lead one to the conclusion that a word processor should be capable of coping with as many as possible of these different eventualities, just as any operating system or language should be flexible enough to cope with most configurations or devices as a matter of course. It is for this reason that whilst word processors which format onscreen (WYSIWYG – What You See Is What You Get) are suitable for short letters and such like, they are not really suitable for customised output. It is important, of course, to have a WYSIWYG facility, but such a facility is not as important as an ability to cope with changed circumstances.

As a simple example, consider a WYSIWYG word processor being used with a proportionally spaced printing device. Some characters are wider than others, so if your text is 60 ordinary characters wide at a maximum, you will probably be able to fit in more than 60 characters, and thus an intelligent word processor should be able to fit in more than 60 characters to a line of printed output. Generally, with a WYSIWYG word processor, all your characters will be of the same width on the screen (unless you have an exceptionally expensive system), and what you see is not what you get.

With PW II, for example, it is possible to enter the widths of your characters in a width table, and then, when you ask for that style of output, PW II uses these widths to calculate the number of characters per line. There are many other PW II features (such as indexing, automatic sectioning, and special environments) which are part of the generalised philosophy, but I have concentrated on the use of the printer because that is the way the output from a word processor reaches the world.

C is for applications

The reason I have looked at an applications package, before I have even given any details of what a C program looks like, is that C is a language for producing applications. The origin of C was not in an academic environment; C was developed in a commercial environment (the Bell Telephone Laboratories) to produce the goods, where the first good was UNIX and other goods were applications programs for a DEC PDP minicomputer.

UNIX and C became very popular in academic circles with those who wished to produce applications and, at a time when the world of commercial computing was strangled by COBOL on large mainframe computers, the UNIX and C scene was considered peripheral to serious commercial programming. It was wrongly believed by those in mainstream commercial computing that UNIX and C were toy systems only fit for small computers and small systems: the real world ran on COBOL and (to a lesser extent) on FORTRAN.

The reason for this misapprehension is that UNIX is an operating system which was developed on small computers, and was not designed to be used with large computers, though obviously there is no reason why it could not be so used.

Academic practitioners often used small DEC computers, and UNIX was developed for a DEC minicomputer: UNIX is not, however, an academic toy – as we have seen. With the increasing use of microcomputers UNIX became attractive to more people because it was designed to optimise the efficient operation of small machines. C, the language for UNIX, was even more attractive because of many useful characteristics derived from its pragmatic parentage. C did not depend on UNIX, and was fairly simple to implement.

We will start our examination of C by looking at Small-C-80, a version of C implemented for microcomputers using CP/M. The particular small machine on which we will study Small-C-80 is the Amstrad CPC464/664.

Chapter Two
Programming in Small-C

Most compiled versions of C follow a similar pattern of operation in moving from source to object code, and nearly all compiled languages which make extensive use of libraries follow the same pattern of operation as C. Teaching languages such as Pascal tend to operate in a different manner, because they were not designed to make extensive use of program libraries.

In this chapter we will examine only one program in particular, a program which makes use of standard function library files, and which uses also a user constructed library file. The superficial purpose of the program is to play a computer game, but the real purpose of the program is to provide us with an opportunity to see how we move from source code to object code in the production of a working C program. As well as studying the implementation of a working program, there will also be a chance to study a few of the main control mechanisms available to the C programmer.

The 'source' program is the name given to the program we write in a programming language to perform our chosen task, and the 'object' program is the source program translated into instructions the computer can use (also known as machine code). To enable us to examine in greater clarity the sequence involved in moving from source program to object code program, we will start with a restricted version of C, that known as Small-C. One advantage of Small-C is that it is generally available on a wide variety of machines.

As C is very much an applications language, we need to discover how at least one real C system operates in practice (as well as in principle), now rather than later. Unless we have a grasp of how a real system operates we are functioning in a vacuum. The beauty of Small-C is that it is not a trivial language, yet its mode of operation is manifest and the system is designed to be comprehensible. The reasoning behind my decision to use Small-C is, therefore, two-fold:

- Small-C is a subset of C, and thus has restricted facilities. However, Small-C has most of the characteristics of a standard C system, and so the flavour of C is not lost. Small-C is a proper (though restricted) version of C.

• Given the way in which Small-C is implemented, each stage of the journey from source code to object code program is easier to appreciate than the similar journey with a version of C designed for use on a larger system. Normally, C on a larger system hides more from the user, because the system aims to make the compilation process less tedious. Small-C is not difficult to use, but is not over-automated.

The version of Small-C I will use for my examples is known as Small-C-80, and was written by John Kershaw. All the examples of Small-C-80 have been executed on an Amstrad CPC computer, running under CP/M.

The original Small-C was designed for use on a computer with an Intel 8080 processor, whereas Small-C-80 is implemented for any computer with the Zilog Z80 processor running under the CP/M operating system. John Kershaw's Small-C-80 is an enhanced version of the classic Small-C system, with improved compilation facilities, though certain standard functions are omitted (such as abs( ), see later). There are several other versions of Small-C available, many of which are in the public domain.

To understand why standard C is so attractive to so many programmers, an explanation of why and how Small-C was developed may help.

Small-C

Small-C was announced to the world by Ron Cain in Dr Dobb's Journal (DDJ) for May 1980. Cain had written an article 'A Small C compiler for the 8080s' in which the first sentence read 'I had to have a compiler for my home computer'.

This was his basic problem, and after a discussion of various avenues he had explored, including the purchase of a 'Tiny-C' interpreter, Cain noted:

> ... the interpreter, though an excellent implementation, was too slow for my needs. Modem to disk programs like to think in terms of microseconds, not milliseconds, and the former was not to be had with an interpreter. The solution was obvious. I had to write the compiler myself. I said obvious, not easy.

An interpreter (such as Tiny-C) differs from a compiler, and it was a compiler that Ron Cain needed. An interpreter translates only a line of program at a time and, once the line has been executed, the interpreter remembers any values of variables but forgets the instructions in that line. Thus an interpreter has to translate a line every time the line is encountered. For example, if a line is repeated 1000 times in a loop, then that line is retranslated on 1000 separate occasions. Generally interactive languages such as APL or LOGO are interpreted (though see later chapters on Instant-C and Living-C).

A compiler takes far longer to translate a program, because each statement is translated (ultimately) into machine code instructions, and the translated instructions are stored (in the case of C) on a disk file. To execute a C program, therefore, the object code is loaded from disk into memory, and then the program in memory is activated. As the complete program has to be translated from source code into object code, the instant response one gets from an interpreted program is not feasible if a program is to be compiled. However, once the translation is finished the compiled program executes far more speedily than an interpreted program because the translation is complete.

The problem of turning a source program into a compiled program (machine code instructions) can be followed from many different directions (and the list below is not exhaustive):

- The translation from source code to object code can be performed by a program originally written in machine code.
- The translation from source code to object code can be performed by a compiled program originally written in a high level language.
- The translation from source code to object code can be performed in two stages:
  a) a program written machine code or a high level language translates the source code into assembly language code
  b) the assembly language code is translated into object code instructions by a standard assembler.

Assembly language is a special form of programming language which is very close to machine code (compare OCODE in BCPL, or P-Code in Pascal – see Appendix A).

The important point to note is that the translation of the source code program is itself performed by a program, though obviously the translation program (the compiler) cannot occupy the same place in memory as the source program.

The Small-C compiler

Cain tried the first of the above techniques (writing the compiler in machine code) but soon stopped. It was at about this point in the proceedings that he realised he was trying to write a compiler for a systems programming language (that is, C) and what better way of writing a compiler than to use a systems programming language?

Tiny-C was a systems programming language, so Cain started to write a compiler for Small-C using the interpreted language Tiny-C. Thus, within the limited memory of his computer (which used an Intel 8080 processor) Ron Cain had to fit the Tiny-C program as well as the compiler he was developing for Small-C. Eventually there came the point at which there was not enough space for the entire compiler to reside in memory along with the Tiny-C interpreter.

Removing comments and shortening variable names reduced the size of the complier, and at last Cain produced a compiler which took a small source program written in C, and turned the program into an 8080 assembly language program. After several refinements, including the use of a C compiler running under UNIX to produce a working Small-C compiler, a C compiler to 8080 assembly language was produced. The compiler was used to produce a further compiler, which highlighted some new errors, then this new compiler was used to generate a further compiler, and so forth.

Cain writes:

> In a nutshell, the compiler:
>
> 1. Is written in C.
> 2. Accepts as input a text file written in C.
> 3. Produces as output a text file of 8080 mnemonics.
>
> The syntax it accepts is a subset of the standard C language.

In the DDJ article is a listing of Cain's compiler program which is itself written in Small-C, where the compiler program was designed to take a source program written in Small-C and turn that source program into an Intel 8080 assembly code program. Unfortunately the Small-C compiler given by Ron Cain still had to be compiled so that the compiler itself could be executed. Cain himself pointed out that the compiler as given in his listing is not directly usable on a system without a C compiler, which seems rather paradoxical. There is a solution to the paradox, however.

The Cain solution is to find a system that runs C (such as a computer which uses the UNIX operating system), enter the program as given in his listing (call it the C_source), compile the C_source using the UNIX C compiler to produce the C_object, and then run the C_object using the listing of the C_source as input. Applying the C_object to the C_source produces the C_assembler, which is an Intel 8080 assembler program listing. The implementer then takes the listing of the C_assembler and puts that listing onto a disk file which is assembled by an 8080 assembler on an 8080 or Z80 computer.

James E. Hendrix in *The Small-C Handbook* (Reston Publishing, 1984) gives an extended version of Small-C which takes Ron Cain's original concept and adds various facilities (to produce version 2.1). Hendrix's book is aimed to appeal to three classes of reader (I quote from Hendrix):

> 1. Small-C programmers who need a handbook on the language and the compiler.

2. Assembly language programmers who wish to increase their productivity and write portable code.
3. Professors and students of computer science. Its small size and the fact that it is written in C instead of assembly language make Small-C an ideal subject for [computer] laboratory projects. Here is a real compiler that is simple enough to be understood and modified by students.

My own reasons for using Small-C are in keeping with points 2 and 3, though they are not exactly the same:

1. I am not writing a reference handbook on Small-C.
2. Small-C is readily available on CP/M and MSDOS, the compiler is not too large (29K for Small-C-80), with facilities for separate compilation, and thus Small-C enables the programmer to develop applications with speed of execution comparable to machine code. Small-C is an excellent method of writing applications, such as database programs, screen editors, or word processors, which need speed of execution but which use little or no floating point arithmetic.
3. Small-C is being used, herein, to show in miniature how a standard C system will operate, and the ways in which the parts of C fit together. This examination will assist the comprehension of information presented in Chapter 3 (What is C?).

For those who would like a deeper understanding and appreciation of Small-C, together with complete reference information, I recommend the book by James Hendrix which, though published in 1984, still uses 8080 code (the 8080 was ten years old in 1984).

Before we leave Ron Cain behind, here is a clear exposition of why C is so important. Cain says of Small-C:

> I've developed the thing about as far as I need to begin using it for the things I originally intended. After all, I did write for a reason.

A Small-C program

The version of Small-C I will use is that developed by John Kershaw for a Z80 based computer (an Amstrad CPC) running under the CP/M operating system. As the Small-C-80 system translates to Z80 assembler mnemonics (and not the 8080 mnemonics of the standard CP/M ASM assembler), the user of Small-C-80 has to have a Z80 assembler available on his machine. There are different systems of mnemonics for assemblers, and the system used by Small-C-80 is that of the Microsoft M80 assembler (MACRO-80) and Microsoft L80 linker (LINK-80). The importance of these two programs will become apparent.

The first version of our example program is:

```
/* hilo in Small-C - Version 1 */

/* Boris Allan               */


#include "stdio.h"

#include "rnd.h"

int attempts, secret, guess;

main()
    {
    random(0);
    attempts = 1;
    secret = random(100);
    scanf("%d", &guess);

    while (guess != secret)
        {
        if (guess < secret)
            printf("\nToo small\n");
        else
            printf("\nToo big\n");

        ++attempts;
        scanf("%d", &guess);
        }

    printf("\nSuccess in %d\n", attempts);
    }
```

The above program is not a particularly apt use of C because hilo is a simple guessing game, and not a systems program by any stretch of the imagination. My excuse for using this program is that we can learn a good deal about the structure of C programs from investigating the development and modification of this particular program. The program is short, but still has all the necessary characteristics of a large program.

The aim of the hilo program is for the computer to 'choose' a secret number at random, and for the user to make a guess about the value of that secret number, to be informed about the relative size of the guess compared with the secret number (that is, large or small). The sequence of guessing, and being told the relative size of the guess compared with the secret number, is continued until the guess is correct (that is, equal to the secret). The number of attempts is then printed on the standard output device.

The title of this section is 'A Small-C program' and that is the problem: we have a program, a source program written in C, and we want to produce an object code program so that we can actually find whether the source program works in the manner we expect. The source program as written is, in effect, a standard C program, but we will use a Small-C compiler (Small-C-80) to produce the object code. Nearly all Small-C programs, unless they have machine specific segments such as assembler directives (using #asm and #endasm), will run under standard C, but not all standard C programs can run under Small-C.

We have an example of a Small-C program, but we have not as yet managed to make the Small-C program operate. The pristine hilo program has to be executed before it really lives: so we now have to make the program live.

Converting Small-C to assembler

The first two lines of the program are commentary; the name of the program and its author (the /* */ lines). The next two lines of program contain the first portions of the real program, that is, instructions which need to be translated into assembler language. These lines are

```
#include "stdio.h"
#include "rnd.h"
```

where STDIO.H and RND.H are two disk files on which there are portions of C source code to be used within the hilo program. The names of the files are enclosed in double quotes for the purposes of generality (this is one of the forms for standard C), even though the quotes are not necessary in Small-C-80.

The first file, STDIO.H, is a standard file on all C systems, though the exact content of the file differs from one computer to another, and from one system to another. The file normally contains information about standard input/output routines, and standard assignments of numbers to names. The .H filetype/extension indicates that STDIO.H is a 'header' file, where the use of .H is not obligatory but is certainly conventional, and thus the RND.H file follows that convention.

RND.H contains C source code to drive the random number generator used in the main( ) function of the above source code. Standard C is a compact language and does not have an inbuilt random number generator, so that a program writer has to provide such a function. The random number function could be given explicitly in the above source code, but – as a random number generator has a certain general utility – the function has been placed in a separate (personal library) file. Even though the above program is very short, we have to be aware that the program is part of a wider program. It is almost impossible to write a C program without the use of a #include, which reflects C's origin as a working systems language.

If the content of the Small-C-80 version of STDIO.H is listed (it is a file containing source code) we can see that STDIO.H is a sequence of instructions to the system, some of which are

```
/* Small-C standard IO header file */
/* Usage is  #include  stdio.h    */

#define STDIN    1    /* standard IO streams */
#define STDOUT   2
#define STDERR   3
#define STDLIST  4

. . . . . . . . . .

extern   int   printf(),   sprintf(),   fprintf(),
               scanf(),    sscanf(),    fscanf();

. . . . . . . . . . .
```

The content of RND.H will be disclosed later, but for now just accept that RND.H contains details of a function random(n), plus a few definitions.

Returning to the program source listing, we declare a function main() which is the key function for any C program. When the C source program is eventually translated into object code and executed, execution of the program starts with the main() function, and if there is no main function then there is no execution. The content of the function extends from the opening brace **(** which follows immediately after the declaration main() to the matching closing brace **)** which comes after the statement 'printf("\nSuccess in %d\n",attempts);'. The details of the mode of operation of the main() function will be examined later, but first we will study how the program is executed.

We have a program written in Small-C, which we have entered and saved to disk as a text file, by use of John Kershaw's excellent CP/M editor (known as MISER). The next step of the process of translation to object code is to take the text file (saved by the editor under the name HILO.C), and transform the contents of that file into some new form, also saved on disk. The first transformation is produced by

sc hilo

where SC is a Small-C-80 program which takes a C source code program, stored as a text (ASCII) file, with the default filetype .C. SC converts that program into a Z80 assembly language program, where the mnemonics are those used by Microsoft for their machine code tools. The particular tool is the Microsoft Macro Assembler MACRO-80 (usually known as M80). The output from SC is a text file HILO.MAC where the filetype .MAC is that expected by the assembler when the file is input to M80. HILO is the root name for the file.

Within the HILO.MAC file, therefore, there is the transformed essence of three files: the main program file (HILO.C) and the two header files (STDIO.H and RND.H). The visible output from the SC program is

```
#include "stdio.h"
End of include file

#include "rnd.h"
random(n)
End of include file

main()
End of main source

No errors found
```

The assembler listing

That the STDIO.H file has been included in HILO.MAC can be revealed by listing the HILO.MAC file (after all, it is a text file), and by comparing the assembler directives with those shown in the listing of STDIO.H. There are certain clear correspondences, for example

```
TITLE     HILO
.Z80

.....

EXT     PRINTF
EXT     SPRINTF
EXT     FPRINTF
EXT     SCANF
EXT     SSCANF
EXT     FSCANF

.....
```

```
MAIN::
    LD      HL, 00
    CALL    RANDOM
    LD      HL, 01
    LD      (C$06+00), HL


  . . . . .
```

It can be seen that the external functions given in the selection from the STDIO.H listing appear exactly in the assembler listing. For example, the EXT PRINTF assembler directive corresponds exactly to the 'extern int printf( )' declaration in STDIO.H. The main( ) function corresponds to the sequence which follows MAIN:: in the assembler listing.

Examining the assembler listing after MAIN:: and comparing its content with that of the C source code reveals certain obvious parallels (there are many less obvious parallels). In the C source there is an instruction to 'random(0)' which appears in the assembler listing as

```
LD      HL, 00
CALL    RANDOM
```

The assembler instructions mean that the HL register pair is loaded with the value 0, and then the routine with the label RANDOM is called. The routine RANDOM expects its parameter value to be available in register HL, and so the value is always placed in this register pair. Later, when there is a call to random(100), the only difference in these two instructions is the value loaded into HL, which has to be 100.

```
LD      HL, 100
CALL    RANDOM
LD      (C$06+02), HL
```

The result of the RANDOM routine is left in the HL register pair, and so in the third line the value in HL is loaded into another location (C$06+02) – a location which corresponds to that occupied by the variable secret (as there is an assignment 'secret = random(100)'). Another assignment is 'attempts = 1' which corresponds to the assembler code

```
LD      HL, 01
LD      (C$06+00), HL
```

That is, load the HL pair with 01, and then store the value in HL in the pair of locations to which (C$06+00) is pointing. When, later in the program, reference is made to the variable 'guess', the location is given as (C$06+04). Collating this information:

```
LOCATION        VARIABLE

(C$06+00)       attempts
(C$06+02)       secret
(C$06+04)       guess
```

and comparing this sequence with the declaration preceding main( )

int attempts, secret, guess;

again shows up the direct correspondence. Each integer in Small-C occupies two bytes of memory, and the variable 'attempts' is the name given in the C source program to those two bytes. In the assembler program, the location which corresponds to the variable 'attempts' is given the label C$06 (or, C$06+00). All the variables in one declaration are stored in sequence, two bytes at a time, and later in the assembler listing there is a directive to set aside 6 bytes starting at location C$06.

Assembling and linking

Note that at this stage the assembler source listing (HILO.MAC) cannot be executed as it stands, because (like HILO.C) the program is not yet in a form which can be understood at the machine code level by the computer. The instructions in the HILO.MAC file have to be changed into such a form by use of the M80 assembler. The command line is

m80 =hilo

which produces yet another file, known as HILO.REL.

Thus far, there are three files: HILO.C, which is the Small-C source program; HILO.MAC, which is the assembler source program; and the new file, HILO.REL, which is a relocatable binary file. The meaning of the term 'relocatable' is that the binary information on the file is so organised that all references to locations in memory are relative references. A relative reference to a memory location is a reference by counting forward or back (that is, go forward or go back a specified number of locations). The relocatable file can thus be placed at any location, and the program can be executed from that location because there are no references to actual (or absolute) memory locations.

A relocatable file may also refer by name to routines and labels outwith the file, and if an attempt is made to execute the file HILO.REL (by changing the filetype to .COM) nothing happens. Nothing happens because the assembler listing refers to many functions (such as SCANF) which appear in the program but are not defined within the program as such: unless it is told how, the program does not know how to SCANF and thus does nothing. The EXTernal functions for input and output are defined in a relocatable file STDIO.REL, and there is another file SCLIB.REL which contains 'library' functions for C other than those used for input/output purposes.

These three relocatable (.REL) files have to be joined together to form the final object code program: the joining together (normally known as 'linking') is performed by Microsoft's L80 (LINK-80) program. In the case of Small-C-80 there is a special program to simplify the linking of files. Known as LINK, the program takes a list of files and links them all together (the SCLIB.REL file is automatically linked and does not have to be specified). When the LINK program is used the root name of the first .REL file provides the root of the object code file (which has a .COM filetype). Thus to produce an object code program HILO.COM which is linked with STDIO.REL and SCLIB.REL we enter

```
link hilo stdio
```

and the output from the program is an object code program file HILO.COM.

On my CP/M system the original source file (HILO.C) occupies ½K, the assembler listing file (HILO.MAC) occupies almost 2K, the relocatable file (HILO.REL) takes up ¾K, and the final object code program file occupies slightly more than 5K (most of which is standard input/output defined by STDIO). To execute the object code program, we enter

```
hilo
```

and the program commences. A specimen sequence of input and output from the program (with program output shown <u>thus</u>) is

```
50
Too big
25
Too small
37
Too small
43
Too small
46
Too small
47
Success in 6
```

Now that we have followed the sequence for creating the HILO.COM object code program we had better find how the program operates.

hilo – Version 1

Ignoring the #include files, the hilo program source is

```
int attempts, secret, guess;          /* 1 */

main()                                 /* 2 */
    {

    random(0);                         /* 3 */
    attempts = 1;
    secret = random(100);
    scanf("%d", &guess);

    while (guess != secret)            /* 4 */
        {
        if (guess < secret)            /* 5 */
            printf("\nToo small\n");
        else
            printf("\nToo big\n");

        ++attempts;                    /* 6 */
        scanf("%d", &guess);
        }

    printf("\nSuccess in %d\n", attempts);
                                       /* 7 */
    }
```

I have added comment numbers (within /* */) to help in the discussion:

1. These are the declarations. There are three variables, of type integer (2 bytes) whose sphere of influence (that is, their 'scope') is global. In other words, they are available for use by any function in the program. If the variables were declared within the function their scope would be local to that function.
2. This declares a function, main( ), which takes no parameters (indicated by the empty parentheses). main is the name of the function for which the C compiler searches when the program is executed, and if main cannot be found then the program cannot be executed.
3. The function random(n) is initialised (by random(0)), and there are initialisations of the integer variables – attempts, secret, and guess.
4. This is the start of a while loop, where the test expression is (guess != secret), and the content of the loop extends from the first { after the test expression to the matching } after 'scanf("%d",&guess);'. The content of the loop is executed while the test expression is true, and in this case the

test is whether the guess does not equal the secret. At the first occasion the test is encountered, guess has been set equal to the value input in the initialisation block /* 3 */, whereas later tests use the value input at /* 6 */.

5. A two-way switch (IF THEN ELSE) which discriminates between the situation where the guess is too small and the situation where the guess is too big. If the guess is equal to the secret then this part of the program is not activated, because the test at the head of the loop means that the content of the while loop is skipped.

6. At the end of the loop there have to be two housekeeping actions: the number of attempts is increased by 1 (that is, ++attempts) and a new guess is input (that is, scanf("%d",&guess);). Control then returns to the beginning of the loop, and the test expression is re-evaluated with the new value of guess. The incrementation operator ++ is more efficient than the equivalent expression 'attempts = attempts + 1' because the action corresponds directly to one machine code instruction.

7. If an exit has been made from the loop, then this expression is evaluated, which is an instruction to print out the text 'Success in', followed by the number of attempts (the %d, as with scanf, means 'expect a decimal number at this point in the proceedings').

An examination of the example program output may help in the understanding of Version 1. We will start to modify the control structures in the source program.

hilo – Versions 2 and 3

The first modification to the hilo program is

```
/* hilo in Small-C - Version 2 */

/* Boris Allan                  */

#include "stdio.h"

#include "rnd.h"

main()
    {
    int attempts, secret, guess;

    random(0);
    attempts = 1;
```

```
secret = random(100);

while (scanf("%d", &guess), guess != secret)
   {
   if (guess < secret)
      printf("\nToo small\n");
   else
      printf("\nToo big\n");

   ++attempts;
   }

printf("\nSuccess in %d\n", attempts);
}
```

The only real differences with this version are that:

- The variables have been moved so that they are now local to the main( ) function. This is far more secure, because only in main( ) can their values be altered.
- An excess 'scanf("%d",&guess);' statement has been removed.

The input request only appears at one point in the program, and serves both to initialise guess (as at /* 3 */ in Version 1) and assign a new value to guess, after each iteration through the while loop (as at /* 6 */). The reduction by one of the number of commands reduces the size of the object code file on disk by 128 bytes (a discernible amount, due mainly to the way in which files are stored in 128 byte chunks in Amstrad CP/M).

Both the commands at /* 6 */ in Version 1 can be introduced into the test expression. Note that the expressions in the test expression are separated by commas to show that they form one unit: the value tested is that of the rightmost expression. ++attempts can be introduced into the test expression if one of the initialisations is modified to 'attempts = 0'.

```
/* hilo in Small-C - Version 3 */

/* Boris Allan                 */


#include "stdio.h"

#include "rnd.h"

main()
   {
   int attempts, secret, guess;
```

```
random(0);
attempts = 0;
secret = random(100);

while (++attempts, scanf("%d", &guess),
      guess != secret)
   {
   if (guess < secret)
      printf("\nToo small\n");
   else
      printf("\nToo big\n");
   }

printf("\nSuccess in %d\n", attempts);
}
```

The while loop structure has three basic aspects:

- Initialisation on entry to the loop for the first time (attempts and secret).
- The test expression (input guess, and then check guess against the secret).
- The loop modification (increase the number of attempts by 1).

These aspects are utilised in Version 4, which demonstrates the action of a for loop.

hilo - Version 4

First examine Version 4, in which there are two major modifications: the while loop is replaced by a for loop, and the RND.H is #included at the end of the file.

```
/* hilo in Small-C - Version 4 */

/* Boris Allan                  */


#include "stdio.h"

main()
   {
   int attempts, secret, guess;

   random(0);

   for (attempts = 1, secret = random(100);
```

```
        scanf("%d", &guess), guess != secret;
        ++attempts)
    {
    if (guess < secret)
        printf("\nToo small\n");
    else
        printf("\nToo big\n");
    }

    printf("\nSuccess in %d\n", attempts);
    }

#include "rnd.h"
```

The result of translating this program to assembler is to produce the following output on screen:

```
#include "stdio.h"

main()

#include "rnd.h"
random(n)
End of include file

End of main source

No errors found
```

This shows that the repositioning of the '#include "rnd.h"' statement has no effect on the translation, other than changing the order within the assembler.

There are three parts to the for loop expression:

1. 'attempts = 1, secret = random(100);' is the initialisation expression (note the comma between the two expressions).
2. 'scanf("%d", &guess), guess != secret;' is the test expression (the test proper is the second of the two expressions).
3. '++attempts' is the loop expression (the contents are executed at each iteration of the loop).

Any of the three parts to the expression may be empty, and a classic DoForever loop is emulated by the combination 'for (;;)'. A variant of this formulation is given in Version 5 (the final version of hilo, you will be glad to discover).

hilo – Version 5

In this version there are two for loops, one (/* 1 */) so that the game can be repeated until we have had enough, and one (/* 2 */) to activate the game itself. There are two other small changes. The first, '#define LIMIT 100', shows how we can increase the generality of any program, in that we use the name of a constant in the program and change the constant's value by use of a #define instruction, if necessary. The second is the use of NULL instead of 0, where NULL has been #defined within STDIO.H.

```
/* hilo in Small-C - Version 5 */

/* Boris Allan                    */


#include "stdio.h"

#define LIMIT 100

main()
    {
    int attempts, secret, guess;

    for (random(NULL);;)                      /* 1 */
        {
        for (attempts = 1, secret = random(LIMIT);
                scanf("%d", &guess), guess != secret;
                ++attempts)                   /* 2 */
            {
            if (guess < secret)
                printf("\nToo small\n");
            else
                printf("\nToo big\n");
            }

        printf("\nSuccess in %d\n", attempts);

        if (getchar() == 'n') break;    /* 3 */

        }
    }

#include "rnd.h"
```

The first loop initialises random(NULL), and does not test or modify (the loop continues forever). The way in which the loop is terminated is by the if test in /* 3 */. The function getchar( ) reads a character from the standard input channnel and that character is compared with the character 'n'. If the character is 'n' then there is a 'break' out of the loop, otherwise (if a number is input) the loop continues to iterate (and another game is played). The inner for loop (/* 2 */) is the one we have met before in Version 4.

Since we keep reusing the function random(n), we had better find what the file RND.H contains.

The RND.H file

The random(n) function returns an integer within the limits 0 to n−1, and operates on a linear congruence method to generate successive members of a series of pseudo-random numbers. The linear congruence method is defined by the relationship

NewValue = (1 + OldValue * Factor) modulo 65536

The equivalent statement in C is

seed = 1 + seed * FACTOR

where seed is declared to be an unsigned integer. An unsigned integer (such as seed) differs from an ordinary integer (such as guess in the main( ) function) in that seed can take values from 0 to 65535, whereas guess can take values from −32768 to 32767. If the result of an unsigned multiplication is greater than 65535, then the result is always taken as modulo 65536.

If a random number is to be constrained within the limits 0 to n−1, then the unsigned random value is taken to modulo n. The modulo operator in C is % and thus the required value is

seed % n

However, we can use a very important feature of C, and one we have used above: any expression in C always delivers a result, and the result delivered by an assignment expression is the value assigned. Thus the required value is produced by

(seed = 1 + seed * FACTOR) % n

where, note, the complete assignment expression is enclosed in parentheses. If we want to remember the value of seed from one call of the function to another, we cannot use an automatic variable whose lifetime is only that of each activation of the function. An automatic variable known as seed would not be the same seed from one call of the function to another.

In some languages the only solution to this problem would be to use global variables (whose values may be modified by any function), whereas in

C we can preserve security by using static variables. These are variables whose existence continues from one call of a routine to another, but whose scope is still local to a particular function. Here is a listing of the RND.H file

```
#define LOCATION 100
#define FACTOR 253

random(n)

    int n;

    {
    static unsigned seed;

    if (n == NULL)
        {
        seed = *LOCATION;
        return;
        }
    else
        if (n < 0) n = -n;

    return((seed = 1 + seed * FACTOR) % n);
    }

#undef FACTOR
#undef LOCATION
```

Two constants are given values; LOCATION is made equal to 100, and FACTOR is made equal to 253: these constants are used to give generality to the content of the function.

The function random(n) has one argument (or parameter): that which is declared immediately after the name of the function

```
    int n;
```

thus the parameter is an ordinary (signed) integer. On entering the body of the function there is a declaration of seed as an unsigned integer, but a special kind of unsigned integer. seed is a static variable, which means that the value of seed the last time the function was called is available for use at the present time (within the life of a program).

As seed is a static variable, and thus does not have to be recreated with each call of the function, the advantage for a random number generator is obvious. There are other advantages because, in addition, static variables are rather more efficient than automatic variables in computational terms. With static variables memory is permanently allocated, and the compiler does not have to reallocate with each call of the function as is the case with automatic variables.

If the argument value is zero/NULL, the function assumes that the seed has to be initialised, and the seed is initialised to the value of the integer 'stored' at the address known as LOCATION (in this case, location 100). If it is known that the value at a specific location varies in a haphazard way, then the #define can be altered so that LOCATION is able to point at a likely address. The * indicates that '*LOCATION' is a pointer to an address, and * is known as a 'unary' operator in this context. That is, where the * and the variable/object are contiguous without a preceding value – in the sequence 'seed * LOCATION', * is a binary operator (meaning multiply). If the seed is initialised then a return is made from the function without specifying a value.

The test is 'n == NULL' and not 'n == 0' because of a desire to be more general, and if the test yields a false result there is a further test 'else if'. The test 'n < 0' is to discover if n is negative, and if n is negative, then the variable is made positive by 'n = -n' (there is no abs( ) function in Small-C-80, but one could easily be written). Once the status of n has been clarified we can then modify the value of the seed, and return a value from the function.

```
return((seed = 1 + seed * FACTOR) % n);
```

This line modifies the value of the seed by multiplying the existing value of the seed by FACTOR and adding 1. The result of the assignment is then modified by taking its value to modulo n (that is, % n) which is the value returned by the function.

After the function definition the LOCATION and FACTOR are undefined, and so can be redefined elsewhere (both LOCATION and FACTOR are popular labels). RND.H is beginning to look like a proper C file.

Chapter Three
What is C?

After examining how the Small-C-80 system works in practice, we will examine the full version of the C language in outline, to get some feel for the form of the language. The version of C to be described in this chapter is that given in *The C Programming Language* by Brian W. Kernighan and Dennis M. Ritchie (Prentice-Hall, 1978) as the version given in 'K&R' is taken to be the 'standard' version of C.

This is a long chapter, but by the end of it you will have covered nearly all there is to know about C, other than how the language is used in practice, which will be the subject of the rest of the book. It may help to study the C syntax given in Appendix C, because this gives the exact form of the language. 'Syntax' is concerned with the correct specification of the language, whereas in this chapter the emphasis is rather more on the 'semantics'. Semantics is concerned with what the language constructs mean, that is, what are the actions produced by these constructs.

Arrays and pointers

The introduction of types into C was a major change from its precursor, the untyped BCPL, but the way in which the types are implemented is still very much in the BCPL style of operation.

In C, an array of five elements (all integer) is declared by

```
int vector[5]
```

where the first element of the five is vector[0], and the final element is vector[4]. Note that the semicolon is used to separate the declaration from the next statement. When the name 'vector' (without any modification) is given in C, a pointer is set up to indicate the location of the first element of the array.

If the size of an array is specified in a declaration, then the size must be a constant value, though it is possible to declare in a function, for example,

```
int vector[];
```

where the implication is that the size of the array is given elsewhere.

We need to distinguish between the address of a location in memory, and the content of that location. The expression 'vector' by itself (that is, without modification) is equivalent to &vector[0], in that vector[0] refers to a location, and the prefix operator & is an injunction to find the address of the location in which the value vector[0] is stored. C allows the declaration of a pointer, where a pointer contains an address: a pointer is indicated by the prefix *, thus a pointer to an integer (pvector) is declared by

```
int *pvector;
```

An integer is normally equal to two bytes on most computers (if the computer's memory is byte oriented; see next section).

Now that pvector has been defined as a pointer, the assignment statement

```
pvector = &vector[0]
```

means that the variable pvector now contains the address of the first element of the vector. Note that an equivalent assignment is

```
pvector = vector
```

and that vector[0] is equal to *vector. As a slight aside on this topic, examine

```
int xvar, yvar;
int *pvar;
pvar = &xvar;
yvar = *pvar;
```

This is equivalent to a simple assignment, but which assignment?

From the declarations we know that there are two integer variables, xvar and yvar, and there is one pointer to an integer variable, pvar. In the first assignment the pointer pvar is set equal to the address of xvar, and in the second assignment yvar is set equal to the value stored at the location to which pvar is pointing. The location, to which pvar is pointing, is the address of the variable xvar, and thus the value stored at that location is the value of xvar. By a circuitous route we have performed the simple assignment

```
yvar = xvar;
```

In fact, the section of code with the pointer effectively mirrors what has to happen when the assignment is translated by the C translator.

We have seen that vector[0] is equivalent to *vector, and this equivalence can be extended. For example, vector[4] is equivalent to *(vector + 4) – remember that *vector is the same as *(vector + 0). Now *(vector + 4) is interpreted to mean the value stored at the address (vector + 4), thus vector[4] actually means the value stored four locations on from the start of the vector. The '+ 4' operation, however, is not quite what it seems: it does not (usually) mean the addition of the number 4 to the address at the start of the vector.

Pointer arithmetic is slightly different from what we might expect because the vector is an integer array and integers are normally two bytes in length. When the C translator encounters the expression 'vector + 4', it realises that the variable 'vector' is a set of integer values, therefore since an integer occupies two bytes, C translates '+ 4' into '+ 4 * 2'. This alteration of the number to be added means that using the expression *(vector + 4) is consistent with the equivalent expression, which is vector[4].

It can be seen that C has taken the idea of indirection from BCPL, and extended the notion to multiple length memory 'cells'. In BCPL the indirection operator is !, which has been generalised in C to provide the pointer operator *, where the pointer operator is always used in a prefix manner in C. In BCPL, for example, to point to element 4 of a vector, one can write vector!4 or !(vector + 4), whereas in C one can only use the prefix form of the operator, that is, *(vector + 4). BCPL's address operator @ correspond to C's & address operator.

Basic types in C

There are very few basic data types in C:

int
This represents an integer in the basic size unit allowed by the computer on which C is implemented. On many computers the size of an integer is equal to two of the basic units (usually bytes of eight bits), but on some larger machines an integer is four bytes. There are varying qualifiers which may be attached to integers:

short int This is an integer which is shorter than the full integer, that is, it occupies fewer memory locations. If an integer is already two bytes, a short integer is usually no shorter, but on some systems where an integer is greater than four bytes there is a difference in extent.

long int A longer integer, occupying a greater number of locations. A long integer is frequently no longer than an integer (it all depends upon the implementation).

unsigned int An integer which is always positive. Thus an unsigned integer will extend from 0 to 65535 on a two byte integer machine, whereas the ordinary integer extends from −32768 to 32767 (in two's complement arithmetic).

Ultimately all you can count on is that a short integer is no longer than an integer is no longer than a long integer. Integers can be expressed in three number systems: decimal (base 10); octal (base 8), where an octal value is distinguished by a leading 0 and there are no negative values; and hexadecimal (base 16), where a hex value is distinguished by a leading sequence 0x and there are no negative values.

char

This is the smallest unit, and is equivalent to one byte on the host computer. The character is stored as an ASCII value from 0 to 255, and thus is always positive. A character variable can be used in arithmetic expressions as if it were a number. For example, if xchar is a character, then

```
xvar = xchar - '0'
```

will store the numerical equivalent of the character value in the integer variable xvar. There are certain specific characters introduced by \ which are known as 'escape' characters. These are usually non-graphic characters, that is, characters which are not usually printed:

\n   Produces a new line/line feed (LF, ASCII 10).
\t   Horizontal tab (HT, ASCII 9).
\b   Backspace (BS, ASCII 8).
\r   Carriage return (CR, ASCII 13).
\f   Form feed (FF, ASCII 12).
\\   Backslash (\, ASCII 92).
\'   Single quote (', ASCII 39).
\"   Double quote (", ASCII 42).
\ooo   Character with ASCII value octal ooo, for example, the backspace is '\10' (octal 10, equal to denary 8).

These escape characters are constants, and not variable quantities.

float

This is a single precision floating point (fractional or real) number. Normally the value is a minimum of four bytes in size, so usually it occupies twice as much storage as an integer. Cunning programmers have been known to use floating point variables as long integers by directly addressing the locations – the world of C is full of inhabitants who use data types for purposes other than those for which they were intended (which takes us back to BCPL...)

double

Intended to be a double precision floating number, this is supposed to occupy twice as many bytes as an ordinary floating point number: sometimes it does, and sometimes it does not ...

There are other types provided by C which are formed by use of pointers, arrays, and a device called a 'struct'. We have met pointers and arrays already, and it should be noted that any of the above primitive types can be made into an array and can, therefore, have a special pointer type – as arrays and pointers are so intertwined.

```
float *pfvar, fvar, fvector[75];
```

declares a pointer, pfvar, to a floating point location, a floating point variable, fvar, and an array of 75 floating point numbers.

Derived types in C

A structure in C is a collection of one or more objects, usually of varying types, where the structure can itself be treated as an object. A structure first has to have a definition, for example

```
struct payment {
    int hours;
    float salary;
    char month[3];
    int year;
};
```

defines a structure with the tag 'payment', which is formed of four main elements. The first element is the hours worked that month (an integer), the second element is the salary (a floating point number), the third element is an array of characters which give the first three letters of the month, and the final element is the year (an integer). If payment was in round units (with no fractional items) then, as all the integers are positive, another way in which the structure might be defined is

```
struct payment {
    unsigned hours, salary;
    char month[3];
    unsigned year;
};
```

We will assume the latter definition of payment.

To declare a variable 'horace', which contains information about a specific person's salary (name unknown), and then to assign to some information to horace we use:

```
struct payment horace;
horace = {37, 4000, "jul", 1990}
```

Note that to enter a string of characters as a unit we use the double quotes; the single quotes are only for single characters. To find the year in which the payment horace is made we select from the structure by use of the dot operator '.', so that

```
horace.month
```

selects the string "jul".

It is possible, of course, to have an array of a structure, and a pointer to a structure. For example

```
struct payment employee[142], *pment;
```

declares an array called 'employee' with 142 elements, and a pointer 'pment' to a payment structure. To select the salary from employee[39], and select the salary from the payment to which *pment is pointing, we use:

```
employee[39].salary
(*pment).salary
```

where the parenthesising of *pment is to distinguish this from the incorrect expression

```
*pment.salary /* incorrect */
```

because the C translator would try to find

```
*(pment.salary) /* incorrect */
```

which is obviously incorrect. Note the use of comments brackets /**/. The clearest way to find the salary of the object to which pment is pointing, is by the special device

```
pment -> salary
pment -> month[0]
```

In the second example the result would be to find the first character of the month for that object. In large-scale C programming a great deal of use is made of structures, and in such programs there is a high frequency of usage for the –> operator.

A further derived type in C is the 'union'. A union is capable of containing one of a variety of objects, where the C compiler keeps track of the possible uses. For example, suppose that a variable needs to contain values from −32768 up to 65535, that is, the range from the lowest value of an integer to the highest value of an unsigned integer

```
union new_int {
    int negint;
    unsigned posint;
} intvar;
```

which defines a union which has two 'fields', that is, negint and posint. The type of negint is int, and the type of posint is unsigned. If a number is negative then it has to be an int (because unsigned ints cannot be negative); if the number is positive then it could be either an int or an unsigned, but if unsigned, then the upper range is higher.

A further 'derived type' is the modification of functions from the default result, which is that a function always returns an integer (see later sections for more about functions). For example, if a function is to return a long integer result, we declare

```
long stretchint(ordint)
int ordint;
{
    long lngint;
    lngint = ordint;
    return(lngint);
};
```

which stretches an ordinary integer to a long integer. (The stretching is accomplished automatically by C, but the function is purely illustrative.)

Type conversions

When objects of different types appear in expressions, the objects are converted to a common type according to specific rules. Conversions are made only if the conversion makes sense: if a floating point number is added to an integer, say, then the integer is converted into a floating point form. The conversion of a double length floating point number to an integer (to index an array) is not automatically performed: 'widening' the type of an object is normally automatic, but 'narrowing' its type is context dependent.

Characters and integers can be mixed freely, because every char is turned into an int. It has to be remembered that a char is always positive, so that if an end of file marker (EOF) returns the value −1, then

```
char cinput;

cinput = getchar();
if (cinput == EOF) ...
            /* check to find end of file */
```

will never be true, because EOF is frequently −1 and a char normally extends in value from 0 to 255. The solution is

```
int cinput;
char cchar;

cinput = getchar();
if (cinput == EOF) ...
            /* check to find end of file */
cchar = cinput;
```

which reads in the character as a signed integer, makes the check, and then assigns the integer value to a character.

In any declaration the format is

```
type_specifier expression
```

where type_specifiers are the 'types' as defined above (plus the 'typedef' declaration). An expression can be fairly complex, as with

```
int (*(*array)[])();
```

which is a pointer to an array of pointers to functions, each returning an integer. Start the decomposition of the declaration as if it were an onion.

```
int xxxx();
```

is the declaration of a function xxxx which returns an integer. The content of xxxx can be expanded to

```
int (*yyyy)();
```

which is a pointer to a function yyyy which returns an integer. Finally, on expanding yyyy, we find that yyyy is an array of pointers, (*array)[]

```
int (*(*array)[])();
```

Thus – as earlier – we find that we have a pointer to an array of pointers to functions. How you would use such a marvellous object is, of course, up to you.

Control structures

There is a distinction in C between statements and expressions. An expression may be loosely defined as something which produces a value. 'xvar' is an expression, as is 'xvar + yvar' or 'xvar == yvar', so that a simple variable is an expression, two expressions added together produce an expression, and a check for the equality of two expressions is also an expression.

What is perhaps even more surprising is that 'xvar = yvar' is also an expression, where the value of the expression is that on the left-hand side. In C there is no special form of assignment statement, and there are many 'assignment' operators (= += -= *= /= %= >>= <<= &= ^= |=, but see later). In most cases statements in C are merely expressions, but there are certain control structures which are statements and not expressions.

Statements are grouped by use of the braces { } , and a series of statements (separated by semicolons) can be used in any situation where a single statement might be used. The braces are the equivalent of pairs of keywords such as begin...end or do...od, and are as easy to understand (and certainly quicker to type). Therefore, whenever a statement is mentioned, remember that it might be a series of other statements enclosed in braces. The basic control mechanisms provided by C are the following, where the term STATEMENT includes a terminating semicolon.

```
if ( EXPRESSION ) STATEMENT
```

```
if ( EXPRESSION ) STATEMENT1 else STATEMENT2

while ( EXPRESSION ) STATEMENT

do STATEMENT while ( EXPRESSION ) ;

for ( <EXPRESSION1> ; <EXPRESSION2> ;
              <EXPRESSION3> ) STATEMENT

switch ( EXPRESSION )
{
   case CONSTANT1 : STATEMENT1
   case CONSTANT2 : STATEMENT2
   .......
   default : STATEMENTd
}

goto IDENTIFIER ;
```

In addition there are two statements, 'break' and 'continue', which are used within control statements.

The if statement comes in two variants: in the first, the statement is evaluated if the expression is 'true' (that is, non-zero), and if false (that is, zero) there is no action; in the second variant there are two statements, the first of which is evaluated if the expression is true and the second if the expression is false. For example, to assign the maximum of two values (corresponding to the variables xvar and yvar) to a variable zvar use:

```
if (xvar > yvar)
   zvar = xvar ;
else
   zvar = yvar;
```

and to check that both xvar and yvar are positive:

```
if (xvar > 0 && yvar > 0)
   if (xvar > yvar)
      zvar = xvar ;
   else
      zvar = yvar;
```

thus we can see how more complex tests can be produced by compounding if statements.

The while statement evaluates the expression and, if true, executes the statement else the control statement is terminated. After the statement has been executed the expression is re-evaluated and, if true, the statement is executed. Control continues until the expression is false. A common use of the while statement is reading from a file:

```
int c ;
c = getchar() ;
while (c != EOF)
{
    .....
    c = getchar()
};
```

or, rather more cunningly:

```
while ((c=getchar()) != EOF)
{
    .....
};
```

A particular form of the while statement is the for statement, where the equivalence is

```
for ( <EXPRESSION1> ; <EXPRESSION2> ;
                   <EXPRESSION3> ) STATEMENT

<EXPRESSION1> ;
while (<EXPRESSION2>)
{
    STATEMENT
    <EXPRESSION3>;
};
```

The <> brackets indicate that the expressions are optional, thus

```
for (;;) { STATEMENT };
```

produces an infinite (DoForever) loop.

The infinite loop can be terminated by use of the break statement, where to execute break means that the loop is exited. break exits only from the immediate control construct (the other constructs for which break can be used are switch, while, and do). break has an affinity with the continue statement: whereas break exits the loop, continue means that the next iteration of the loop is commenced. Continue does not, of course, apply to switch.

Instead of the while loop to read in characters, we might try

```
for (;;)
{
    c = getchar() ;
    if (c == EOF) break ;
    .....   };
```

though one advantage of the while loop is that the test is explicit, and not hidden away in the body of the loop. A further form of the for loop which may be used is

```
for (;(c = getchar()); != EOF)
{
    ......
};
```

It is possible for the expression to be compound, so that to set indx to zero and list[0] to zero, plus a few checks, we can write:

```
for (indx = 0, list[0] = 0 ;
    indx < 10 ;
    ++indx, list[indx] = indx)
{
......
};
```

To work out what happens with the above loop, you will need to know that the ++ operator means increment by 1, so that ++indx is the same as indx =indx+1. The above loop sets indx to zero and list[0] to zero, then checks to see if the indx is less than 10. If it is less than 10 then the compound statement within braces is executed. At the end of the compound statement the indx is incremented by 1, and the value of the array element list[indx] is set equal to indx.

Here is how to perform a typical loop for values of i from 0 to N − 1:

```
for (i = 0 ; i < N ; ++i)
{
.....
};
```

The test for both the while and for loops is at the top of the loop, in that the loop will not be executed if the test gives a false result. A test at the end of the loop (almost like a negative 'until') is performed by the do loop:

```
do
{
    scanf("%d", &number)
    ...
}
while (number != 0) ;
```

This section of code reads in a decimal integer ("%d") and stores the result of the read into a location whose address is given by &number (that is, the value is stored in the variable number); some code (...) is then executed and, if the number is not equal to 0, then the loop is repeated.

At times we may wish to search through a set of fixed alternatives: this task is performed by use of the switch statement (first introduced by BCPL). Suppose we wanted to separate out the number of even digits in a file from the number of odd digits.

```
main()   /* odd, even, and other */
{
    int inchar, oddnum, evennum, otherchar ;
    oddnum = evennum = otherchar = 0 ;

    while ((inchar = getchar()) != EOF)
        switch (inchar)
        {
            case '0' :
            case '2' :
            case '4' :
            case '6' :
            case '8' :
                ++evennum ;
                break ;
            case '1' :
            case '3' :
            case '5' :
            case '7' :
            case '9' :
                ++oddnum ;
                break ;
            default :
                ++otherchar ;
                break;
        }
    printf("\nodd = %d, even = %d, other = %d\n",
        oddnum, evennum, otherchar) ;
}
```

Note the use of break to exit from the construct so that each set of case labels is treated as a distinct entity. If there was no break after ++evennum, for example, control would fall through to the next set and the program would also increment ++oddnum. The character '\n' is the linefeed/newline command.

Strictly speaking, there is no need for the break after default because that is the last label in the switch. The break label is needed for security purposes, as it is always possible that another label or set of labels was added after the default sequence. The cases and default can occur in any order.

Values, operators, and expressions

Expressions and operators have certain specific priorities and can be conveniently grouped into primary operators, unary operators, binary operators, assignment operators, and the comma. Primary operators have the highest priority, unary operators next highest, the binary operators have lower and varying priorities, assignment operators all have the same lower priority, and then there is the comma.

Primary operators

These all have the same priority, and are evaluated from left to right.

( )   Parentheses, used in various contexts.
[ ]   Square brackets, used for array element selection.
.   Dot, field selector used with structures and unions.
$->$ Structure pointer to field.

Unary operators

These are operators which take only one expression. Usually the operators are prefix, but sometimes they can be postfix. The order of evaluation is from right to left.

*   Pointer to the content of the expression treated as an address, prefix.

&   Provides the address of its expression, prefix.

−   Changes sign of expression, prefix.

!   Changes logical state to 1 if expression is equal to 0, or to 0 if expression is non-zero, prefix.

~   Changes every bit in expression to reverse value, for example ~10 is 01; also known as one's complement, prefix.

++   Adds 1 onto expression. If used in prefix manner, then the expression is incremented before its value is used, but if postfix then the value is used before expression is incremented.

−−   Subtracts 1 from expression. If used in prefix manner, then the expression is decremented before its value is used, but if postfix then the value is used before expression is decremented.

sizeof( ) Produces size in bytes of the value produced by expression, prefix.

(TYPE)   A prefix operator which changes the type of expression to the type designated within parentheses. For example, if a function expects an integer and the expression nfloat is floating point, then we can use

```
function((int) nfloat)
```

to make sure that the conversion is performed. The technical name for the forced conversion of an expression is a 'cast'.

Binary operators

These operators have varying priorities within this category. The priorities are given in the following order:

```
*    /    %
+    -
>>   <<
<    >    <=    >=
==   !=
&
^
¦
&&
¦¦
?:
```

Some of these operators may be obvious, but some are not, so here are brief explanations:

* / %	The multiplication, division, and remainder/modulus operators.
+ −	The addition and subtraction operators.
>> <<	Shift right and shift left. $x >> 2$ will shift x right by 2 bits (x being treated as a binary number). Shift left by 1 (that is, $x << 1$) is equivalent to a multiplication by 2, and a shift right by 1 ($x >> 1$) is equal to a division by 2, with no remainder. For a left shift the vacant bits are replaced by zeros, but for a right shift the way in which the bits are filled for signed quantities depends on the computer implementation.
<> <= >=	Less than, greater than, less than or equal to, and greater than or equal to, comparison operators.
== !=	Comparison operators for equal to, and not equal to. It is very easy to write = rather than == so take care: if (c = 4) { } will be evaluated to 4, and thus the statement will always be activated, whereas we probably meant if (c == 4) { } which is a different test.
&	The bitwise AND operator (not to be confused with the logical AND, &&).
^	The bitwise XOR (eXclusive OR) operator.
¦	The bitwise OR operator (not to be confused with the logical OR, ¦¦).
&&	The logical AND connective (not to be confused with the bitwise AND, &).

¦ ¦	The logical OR connective (not to be confused with the bitwise OR, ¦).
?:	Not really a binary operator, but an ternary operator used in the form EXPRESSION1 ? EXPRESSION2 : EXPRESSION3. The truth status of the EXPRESSION1 is evaluated and, if true, EXPRESSION2 is activated, otherwise EXPRESSION3 is activated. For example, to assign the larger of two values A or B to the variable X, we can use

```
X = (A > B) ? A : B ;
                /* X is the max of A and B */
```

which is a very neat way of performing the operation. It is also known as the conditional operator.

All the above binary operators group from left to right.

Assignment operators

Assignment operators are used in expressions which produce a value, the value being that assigned to the variable on the left-hand side of the operator. In the following, LHS stands for left-hand side of the expression, and RHS stands for the right-hand side.

=	Makes the LHS equal to the value of the RHS.
+=	Takes the value on the RHS, adds it to the value of the LHS, and assigns the sum to the LHS.
−=	Takes the value on the RHS, subtracts it from the value of the LHS, and assigns the result to the LHS.
*=	Takes the value on the RHS, multiplies it by the value of the LHS, and assigns the result to the LHS.
/=	Takes the value on the LHS, divides it by the value of the RHS, and assigns the result to the LHS.
%=	Takes the value on the LHS, divides it by the value of the RHS, and assigns the remainder to the LHS.
<<=	Takes the value on the LHS, shifts it left by the value of the RHS, and assigns the result to the LHS.
>>=	Takes the value on the LHS, shifts it right by the value of the RHS, and assigns the result to the LHS.
&=	Takes the value on the LHS, performs a bitwise AND with the value of the RHS, and assigns the result to the LHS.
^=	Takes the value on the LHS, performs a bitwise XOR with the value of the RHS, and assigns the result to the LHS.
¦=	Takes the value on the LHS, performs a bitwise OR with the value of the RHS, and assigns the result to the LHS.

All assignment operators group from right to left.

Functions in C

A C program consists of one or more files containing function and data declarations: in a sense, therefore, a program is a sequence of declarations. The actions of the program are produced by executing statements within functions. Execution is commenced when the system calls the principal function, known as 'main'.

A 'declaration' describes the properties of an object (its type), whereas a 'definition' not only declares a variable but also allocates storage or (for a function) provides the executable code.

A 'function' in C corresponds to both the subroutines and procedures of other languages, and to what are usually known as functions. Subroutines normally have an action but do not produce a value, whereas functions are used principally to produce a value. A function in C has an action, and returns a value if so programmed. The format of a function is

```
<type> funcname( <parameters> )
<declarations>
{
compound_statement
}
```

Thus a function may (optionally) have its type specified (the type of the value returned by the function); always has a function name, with (optional) parameters being enclosed in parentheses; may (optionally) have declarations of objects whose scope is specific to the function; and has a compound statement, enclosed in braces, which specifies the action of the function.

The parameters are optional but, even if the parameters are not used, the parentheses are still necessary, the most obvious case being the main() function. Parameters are passed by 'value', which means that whatever happens to a variable within a function definition it does not affect the value of that variable outside the function. If the main function has parameters this means that these parameters are assumed at runtime, i.e. when the compiled program is activated at the system level we can introduce options to the program.

For example, a program might be known as 'copyfile', and to copy from file xxxx to yyyy we enter

```
copyfile xxxx yyyy
```

at the command level. Within the C program we have a declaration of a main function, and two parameters

```
main(argc, argv)
int argc;
char *argv[];
```

The number of command line parameters is given by the integer argc. Note that this name is conventional, and should not be altered because all C systems have special functions for interpreting command line input, which assume this name. The pointer *argv[ ] is equivalent to argv[ ][ ], or an array of an array of characters (that is, an array of strings). argv[0] is actually the string corresponding to the program name (that is, "copyfile"). argv[1] is "xxxx" and argv[2] is "yyyy".

This system is consistent with the UNIX philosophy of the sequencing of commands, a feature (piping) which also appears in some other operating systems. For example, those who have used MSDOS or PCDOS will recognise that this is the way in which batch programs in MSDOS name their parameters (with the program name being parameter zero, that is, %0). This is not surprising because MSDOS has many explicit UNIX/C language features. One strange feature of MSDOS, however, is the way in which command lines are treated in C: in MSDOS it is not possible to address argv[0] because this information is not available from MSDOS. It is possible to address argv[1] onwards, but not the program name.

The C decision always to call parameters by value produces a more secure programming environment, but calling by value also has a few problems. For example, consider a function to read in a value and store the value in a variable xvarint. The function is used in this manner

```
readin(xvarint) ; /* does not work */
```

where we then use the new value of xvarint in our computations. This function will not work, cannot work, because its value cannot be modified by any function. If you think back to the use of pointers and addresses, you may remember that xvarint is equivalent to *(&xvarint), which means that xvarint by itself is equivalent to the value contained in the location &xvarint. The address of xvarint (&xvarint) never alters, so if the address is passed as a value, it is possible to change the contents at that location.

It is for this reason that the standard function scanf( ) uses an address as a parameter value, thus to read a value into xvarint we use

```
scanf("%d", &xvarint) ;
            /* xvarint is a decimal integer */
```

so that, by passing an address, we can alter the content of the location at &xvarint. For this technique to be successful, the function declarations (immediately after the parameters) have to include pointer declarations.

A common example to illustrate this point is that of the function to swap two values, but here is an example which changes a distance given in feet (fdist) to a distance expressed in US nautical miles (mdist), and kilometres (kdist).

```
nasa(fdist, mdist, kdist)
     /* change feet into other units */
float *mdist, *kdist ;
{
   *mdist = fdist / 6076.1033 ;
      /* US measure, as used on Space Shuttle */
   *kdist = fdist / (3.0 * 0.9144) ;
      /* UK standard */
}
```

To convert 10000 feet to US nautical miles, storing the result in 'Maui', we use nasa(10000, &Maui, &temp). The float type description may be used with the function to return a floating point value if only the distance in US nautical miles is required (that is, without any need for the metric measure)

```
float NASA(fdist)
{
   return fdist / 6076.1033 ;
}
```

One other very helpful use of address parameters and (thus) pointers comes with modifying structures. Returning to the example

```
struct payment
{
   unsigned hours, salary;
   char month[3];
   unsigned year;
};
```

and the declaration

```
struct payment employee[142] ;
```

suppose we would like to use a function which will allow us to change employee records, by entering the employee designation and the values.

```
change_payment(empadd, hrs, sal, mo, yr)
     /* alter salary information */
struct payment *empadd ;
char mo[] ;
{
   empadd->hours = hrs ;
   empadd->salary = sal ;
   copy(mo, empadd->month) ;
   empadd->year = yr;
}
```

```
copy(stringa, stringb)
      /* function to copy strings */
char stringa, stringb ;
{
    int indx ;
    indx = 0 ;
    while ((stringb[indx] = stringa[indx])
          != '\0') /* '\0' is end of string */
        ++indx ;
}
```

The copy() function uses an interesting test:

stringb[indx] = stringa[indx]

which assigns the value contained in the location denoted by string a[indx] to the location denoted by stringb[indx], leaving the value of the expression as stringb[indx]. Let this expression be shown as xxxx, so that the next portion is

xxxx != '\0'

which tests to see if xxxx (that is, stringb[indx]) is not equal to the character '\0'. The '\0' character is the end of string marker (or null) and its actual value is zero (0).

Data and scope

Objects in C not only have a type but also have a storage class. The storage class indicates when objects come into existence and when they disappear. The shorthand for these 'scope' declarations is

```
static
extern
auto
register
typedef
```

where the last decalaration is of a different nature from the other declarations. The meanings of these terms are as follows.

Static variables
If objects are declared at the 'top level', that is, the declarations are outside of any function definition (including main()), then these objects are static in that they exist throughout the execution of the program. Static variables may be local to a function if so defined. For example, a seed in a

random number generator needs to be constant from one activation to another, so

```
static int seed ;
```

will mean that the value will be kept from one activation to another, even though all the other variables are automatic. Top level objects (variables and functions) which are explicitly declared as static cannot be used by programs from other files.

External variables

These are static variables which can be accessed by programs from other source files. That is, all references to an external variable named xxxx are references to the same object, from wherever the reference is made. At the top level (outside all functions) the default nature for a declaration is extern (short for external).

Automatic variables

Variables which are declared within the body of a function (without modification) are known as automatic variables, that is, they come into existence when the function is entered and disappear when the function is exited. It is possible to declare automatic variables as being register variables. Inside a function, the default nature for a declaration is 'auto' (short for automatic).

Register variables

These are automatic variables, and the declaration of a variable as register is an indication to the C compiler (which may be ignored) to place these variables in machine registers. No actual registers are mentioned, and the indication may be ignored.

Typedef identifiers

Declarations whose 'storage class' or 'scope' is typedef do not, in fact, define a type of storage, rather an identifier is defined which can then be used in place of a type description. For example

```
typedef float income;
income janet;
```

will define a 'type' (which is, in fact, a floating point number) but allow you to give the type the name income. This means that a program is slightly more readable. A better example is when the typedef is used to name a structure

```
typedef struct {float val1, val2} point,
           complex ;
point origin = {0, 0} ;
complex zero = {0, 0} ;
```

typedefs are not greatly used in C programming, because #define is often used in place of the name. However, in the case of the point and complex structures, the similarity between the two concepts is so strong that it makes sense to define them in this manner – to reinforce the equivalence of the concepts.

Declarations may appear at the top level or at the head of a compound statement (a block). Declarations in an inner block temporarily override those of identically named variables outside the block. The scope of a declaration persists until the end of its block, or until the end of the file (if the declaration was at the top level).

As function definitions are possible only at the top level there are no internal functions (that is, no function definition may be nested within another definition).

C preprocessor

Before the interpretation of any C program, certain aspects of the environment need to be clarified. Any line beginning with a # is an instruction to what is termed the preprocessor. Situated at the beginning of the file being translated, the preprocessor has three main tasks; macro substitution (or token replacement), the inclusion of designated files, and conditional compilation.

The preprocessor allows the substitution of values for specific identifiers in a program. For example, suppose we need some standard constant in a program, but for the purposes of clarity (and possible later modification) we wish to use the label GRAVITY throughout the program whenever we need the value 9.80665 metres per second squared (the acceleration due to gravity in Internatioanl Standard Units). Note that the #define statement does not end with a semicolon, and only extends over one line. The statement

```
#define GRAVITY 9.80665
```

would define a constant known as GRAVITY so that whenever we use GRAVITY in the program the value 9.80665 will be substituted. Note that the name is given in upper-case; this is a C convention (and only a convention) employed because the use of upper-case helps identify constants. A useful token which can be used to control execution is DoForever (not a constant):

```
#define DoForever for (;;)
```

or (using the while construct)

```
#define DoForever while (1)
```

The use of such a construction will take the form

```
DoForever
{
    .....
}
```

It is by extensive use of the preprocessor that the full range of BCPL control structures can most easily be implemented.

A general print statement for one variable can be defined by a macro name with parameters, for example

```
#define PRINT(style,value)
        printf("Output is %style \n", value)

/* Note the above is over one line and not on */
/* two lines. The only reason the above is */
/* shown on two lines is the constraint of */
/* line length */
```

and to output a decimal number, prefaced by 'Output is':

```
PRINT(d,5)
```

where the 'style' (for example, 'd') is one of the standard output formats for printf (see the next section on 'The C environment').

At any time the command

```
#undef DoForever
```

will forget the definition of DoForever.

If there is a statement of the form

```
#include "FileName"
```

then the complete contents of the file FileName are inserted in the program at that point. A search is made for the file in the current disk directory and, if not there, the search is continued through a series of 'standard places' (to quote K&R). If the statement is

```
#include <FileName>
```

only the standard places are searched, and not the current directory (the directory in which the source file is situated). The #included files may have #include statements (in standard C).

There are three forms of test which are used to decide whether a sequence of actions is to be activated (that is, conditional compilation):

#if constant_expression   Checks to see whether the expression evaluates to a non-zero value.

#ifdef identifier_name   Checks to see whether the identifier named has been defined already in the preprocessor.

#ifndef identifier_name   Checks to see whether the identifier named has not been defined in the preprocessor, or has been #defined and then #undefined.

If true any statements following the test are treated as standard program text in compilation, until an #else or #endif. If the condition is untrue then the text after the #else statement (if present) is used in compilation until the #endif statement is encountered. There are other special preprocessor commands for 'conditional compilation' which are implementation dependent (for example #asm and #endasm for assembler segments).

Since many diagnostics refer to line numbers, there exists a method to specify a set of standard line numbers:

#line constant_identifier

which enables both consistent numbering of source code from many different files and simplified communication of information about bugs, because the line numbers are consistent from application to application.

The C environment

The designers of C (taking their cue from BCPL) decided to confine the C language to facilities which have a close correspondence with machine operations (and thus machine intructions). This explains why there are no complex provided types in C, so that if you want a complex type you have to take responsibility for its construction.

This cleanness of the C data types, for example, means that the user has to be rather more aware of how it is possible to affect the machine environment. Any C system should always provide access to the primitive system calls when a close interaction is desired, but fortunately there are various standard library functions for each version of C which aim to promote portability of code whilst keeping close to the machine. The standard library facilities are concentrated on the areas of storage allocation, string handling, and input/output. Although there is a 'standard' library, it is as well to check on the content of your system's library.

The more common facilities tend to be concentrated on the input/output facilities and string handling facilities.

Input/output
getchar( )
Read a character (actually an ASCII value) from the standard input device (remember to assign the result to an integer).

putchar(c)
Puts the character c on the standard output device (as an ASCII value).

printf(control_string, arg1, arg2, ...)
printf converts, formats, and prints its arguments on the standard output channel under the direction of the control_string. There are two types of element in the control_string: the control characters (given above) and ordinary characters, and then the conversion specifications.

The conversion specifications are introduced by the character and ended by a conversion character. Between the % and the conversion character there may be certain specific codes.

1. A minus sign, which specifies that the argument should be left justified within its field.
2. A digit string specifying the minimum field width; the converted number will be printed in a field at least this number of bits wide. If the number is too small the field will be padded, and if the number is too large it will overflow the field (and still be printed).
3. A stop (.) used to separate the field width (left) from the digit string (right).
4. The digit string (the precision) which specifies the maximum number of characters to be printed by a string, or the number of digits to be printed to the left of the decimal point for a float or double.
5. A length modifier (l) which indicates that the item is a long integer rather than a simpler integer.

The conversion characters are:

d   Convert argument to decimal notation.
o   Convert argument to unsigned octal notation (without a leading zero).
x   Convert argument to unsigned hexadecimal notation (without a leading 0x).
u   Convert argument to unsigned decimal notation.
c   Argument is single character.
s   Argument is string: characters from the string are printed until a null character is reached, or until the number of characters specified by the precision is exceeded.
e   Argument is either float or double, and is converted to decimal notation in the form $<->$m.nnnnnnE$<+/->$xx where the length of the string of ns is specified by the precision. The default precision is 6.
f   Argument is either float or double, and is converted to decimal notation in the form $<->$mmm.nnnnnn where the length of the string of ns is specified by the precision. The default precision is 6 (note that the number of digits before the decimal point is independent of the precision).
g   Use %e or %f, whichever is shorter; non-significant zeros are not printed.
%   %% is printed as %%.

scanf(control_string, arg1, arg2, ...)
All arguments to scanf( ) have to be passed as addresses, so that the value may be returned. There are many similarities with printf( ). The control_string is a sequence of indicants enclosed in quotes. An indicant is a %, then possibly a number to give the maximum field width or * to indicate that the field is to be skipped, and then a conversion character.

d   A decimal integer is expected, the corresponding argument has to be a pointer (an address).

o   An octal digit (with or without a leading zero) is expected, the corresponding argument has to be a pointer (an address).

x   A hexadecimal integer (with or without a leading 0x) is expected, the corresponding argument has to be a pointer (an address).

h   A short integer is expected, the corresponding argument has to be a pointer (an address).

c   A single character is expected, the corresponding argument has to be a pointer (an address), and the next input character is placed at the pointer address. To read the next non-white character use %1s (as the space is itself a character).

s   A character string is expected, the corresponding argument has to be a pointer (an address) which indicates an array of characters large enough to accept the string and the terminating null \0, which will be added.

f   A floating point number is expected, the corresponding argument has to be a pointer (an address). The input format for a float is an optional sign, a string of numbers possibly including a decimal point, and an optional exponent field with E or e followed possibly by a signed integer.

e   A synonym for f.

sprintf(string, control_string, arg1, arg2, ...)
sscanf(string, control_string, arg1, arg2, ...)
These two functions act exactly as printf( ) and scanf( ) but place the result in the named string (which has, of course, to be large enough to take the output).

Accessing files
It is a very limited system that only uses standard input and output channels, and within the standard library there is a definition of a FILE type. Thus to open a file FileName, we use a pointer to a file (in a similar way to the use of a pointer for a string), and use the standard function fopen(name, mode) which returns a pointer to the appropriate file. That is

```
FILE *fopen(), *filepointer ;
filepointer = fopen(FileName, "r") ;
```

makes fopen( ) return a pointer to a FILE, with filepointer being a pointer to a FILE. The filepointer is then made equal to the pointer returned when FileName is opened for reading ("r", the other modes being write "w", and append "w"). If there is an error then fopen( ) will return the null pointer value NULL (or zero).

To read in the next character from the file FileName we use

```
c = getc(filepointer) ;
```

or to write to a file to which FP is pointing

```
putc(c, FP) ;
```

When a program is commenced, three files are opened automatically with special file pointers: the pointers are stdin (standard input), stdout (standard output), and stderr (standard error output). The getchar( ) and putchar(c) functions can be considered to be defined as

```
#define getchar() getc(stdin)
#define putchar(c) putc(c, stdout)
```

These standard files are normally assigned to the terminal/console, but stdin and stdout may be assigned to other files or devices. stderr cannot be reassigned, and thus error output always goes to the terminal.

Two further functions are fgets(input_line, MAXLINE, FilePointer), which reads the next input line (including the newline) from the file FilePointer, when up to MAXLINE-1 characters are read into the string input_line. Normally fgets also returns the input_line, and at the end of file NULL is returned. fputs(output_line, FilePointer) outputs a string (output_line) to the file with which FilePointer is associated.

There are various less commonly used facilities in the standard library, which are still worth noting. These facilities include ungetc(c, FilePointer) which 'pushes' a character c back onto the file associated with FilePointer and system(string) which takes a system command given as the parameter string and executes the command (control returns to the program). A more advanced command is calloc(n, sizeof(type_designation)) which is a function that returns a pointer to the start of the memory allocated as n items of the sizeof(type_designation); if the function is assigned to the pointer cp then cfree(p) releases the space allocated.

Small-C modifications

The best (and highly excellent) description of Small-C is by James E. Hendrix, *The Small-C Handbook* (Reston Publishing, 1980); the Small-C-80 compiler introduced in Chapter 2 conforms to the general description in Hendrix. If a feature of Small-C is incompatible with standard C but Small-C accepts the standard C format for that feature, then I will not give the specific Small-C variant. If, however, a standard C feature will not work on Small-C, then I give that feature.

1. Implementations of standard C tend to use the linefeed character for a newline, whereas Small-C implementations often use carriage return. To save problems of compatibility it is always safer to use '\n' than the ASCII value.

2. Small-C assumes that an undeclared name refers to a function, whereas this is only assumed by standard C if the name appears as function call. For this reason try to avoid referring to undeclared functions except in function calls.

3. Small-C always assumes that integer constants are decimal, so that a leading zero is not taken as denoting an octal number, as it is in standard C. Leading zeros should therefore be avoided, to save any possible confusion.

4. Small-C only allows the digits 0..7 in an octal escape sequence, whereas standard C considers 8 to be octal 10, and 9 to be octal 11.

5. Small-C indicates to called functions how many arguments are being passed, but standard C does not.

6. Small-C uses file descriptors to identify files where as standard C uses pointers, though by use of the fopen function or the symbols stdin, stdout, and stderr compatibility can be maintained.

7. There are no structures (and, thus, no $->$).

8. There are no floating point numbers.

9. Declarations which involve multiple levels of pointer addressing are not allowed, for example

```
int *array[] ;
```

though muliple levels are allowed in expressions.

10. There is no conditional expression, for example ((a != 0)? a : b).

11. Functions can only deliver an int.

12. Macros cannot take parameters.

13. Short variable names may cause confusion with the Z80 assembler.

14. Pointers may not be initialised.

15. Non-intialised declarations do not default to zero.

Chapter Four
Microsoft C

The next chapter is devoted to developing a translator for a simple programming language. The language is aimed at providing an interactive system for arithmetical computation, with facilities for the use of variables (to be known as Varith).

The system is to be implemented in Microsoft C (or MC). One reason for developing a translator in Microsoft C is that such a project helps explain some characteristics of C compilers such as that from Microsoft. Before we progress with the development of our translator we need to know something about the MC compiler we will be using to create the Varith translator.

MC works under two main disk operating systems, MSDOS and XENIX (see Appendix B), and the programs in this chapter were executed on an IBM-compatible PC (the Advance 86B with 256K RAM) running under MSDOS Version 2.11. There are three standard memory 'models' (small, medium, and large, depending on the memory requirements for program and data); the Varith translator was written for the small memory model.

A complete explanation of the workings of MSDOS are beyond the scope of this text, but those without an MSDOS PC need not worry because such a complete explanation is not necessary. I will, however, give sufficient explanation of the necessary aspects of MSDOS to show how C fits in with the operating system. When you have finished this chapter it might be a good idea to read Appendix B on UNIX.

The software provided for the MC compiler consists of three main categories of files.

Executable files

These files are a special category of MSDOS file, distinguished by the extension (filetype) .EXE, which means that such files contain relocatable programs which are executed by giving the main name for the file. The .COM files of CP/M are programs, but they are not relocatable in that the .COM programs can only be executed from one specific location. The .EXE files include, amongst other things:

MSC.EXE

This is the normal MC control program for the compiler (compare CL.EXE), and the program is run by entering MSC. The four compiler stages (or 'passes') are executed in order by this program (that is, P0.EXE P1.EXE P2.EXE P3.EXE).

P0.EXE

The program to run the preprocessor (that is, the inclusion of extra files) initiated by #include commands, and the translation of other instructions beginning with #. This program therefore includes all relevant files and makes all relevant macro substitutions without trying to make any sense of the program. P0 is the first pass of the compiler.

P1.EXE

The program to run the language parser, that is, checking the program for sense, and turning the program instructions into a special form suitable for analysis at the next stage (by P2.EXE). This program comprises the second pass of the compiler.

P2.EXE

The program to run the object code generator, that is, the converted (parsed) source program (of the second pass) is converted into machine instructions. Some references to to global variables and functions are undetermined, and cannot be resolved until linking at a later stage. The P2 program forms the third pass of the compiler.

P3.EXE

The program to run the optimiser, link text emitter and the assembly listing generator, that is, the object code is further modified in the interests of efficiency, the new object code is made available for linking, and the assembly code can be listed for comparison with the original source code program. This is the fourth pass of the compiler.

LINK.EXE

The program to run the Microsoft linker utility LINK, that is, compiled object code files are linked together and an executable code run file is output. The resulting file is not restricted to specific memory addresses, and can be loaded and executed by the operating system at any convenient address (up to 1M of code and data).

LIB.EXE

The program to run the program library management utility LIB, that is, the creation, organisation and maintenance of run-time libraries. A run-library is a collection of compiled or assembled functions that provides a common set of useful routines. A program can call a run-time routine as if it were defined within the program by linking a run-library file and searching for the function in the library file. Run-time libraries are are created by combining separately compiled object files into one library file, usually with the extension .LIB (though other extensions are admissible).

CL.EXE
An alternative control program for running the compiler (compare MSC.EXE), provided for those who are used to the CC command used in XENIX or UNIX systems (see Appendix B). The MSC program only invokes the four passes, whereas with CL one can also invoke the linker (LINK).

EXEPACK.EXE
EXEMOD.EXE
These are special programs used to modify executable program files, well beyond our remit.

The executable program files can be compared with those of Small-C and it can be seen that, in general, there are strong and clear correspondences – even though the MC system is necessarily more complex. It is suggested (in the Microsoft documentation) that all the .EXE files be placed in a \BIN subdirectory, so that to refer to the MSC program we use

\BIN\MSC.EXE

This subdirectory (\BIN) corresponds to the standard subdirectory for object code programs in UNIX.

Include files

These are text files which can be incorporated into a program by use of the preprocessor directive #include. These files contain definitions and declarations used by the functions in run-time library files. The contents of the #include files range from console input/output functions to string manipulation functions, and there are two main types of #include file. There are the standard #include files which Microsoft suggest be kept in an \INCLUDE subdirectory, for example

\INCLUDE\ASSERT.H

and the 'system' #include files which, for consistency with UNIX and XENIX, are placed in a subdirectory \INCLUDE\SYS where, for example, the #include file which declares types used for file status and time information is fully described by

\INCLUDE\SYS\TYPES.H

These files are supposed to contain system level definitions, though many files in this subdirectory do not, but as SYS is commonly used in XENIX and UNIX this convention is maintained.

Library files

These files contain run-time library routines to be linked with a program. A complete set of library routines is provided for each of the three memory models, plus two files EM.LIB and 87.LIB for use with any memory model. EM.LIB is a floating point emulator used to perform floating point operations, and 87.LIB is the 8087/80287 floating point library (the 8087 and 80287 are special numerical coprocessors for use with the 8086/8088/ 80186 processors and the 80286 processor respectively).

The compiler uses the emulator (EM.LIB) by default, unless either the library file 87.LIB is specified (in which case the 8087/80287 is needed) or the library file SLIBFA.LIB is specified (SLIBFA.LIB accentuates the speed of computation rather than the precision of results). Whenever the program uses EM.LIB or 87.LIB then the floating point library SLIBFP.LIB is required. Note that extra libraries are needed to perform floating point calculations.

When a program is compiled using MSC.EXE or CL.EXE the compiler inserts the names of the standard library (SCLIB.LIB) and the default floating point libraries (EM.LIB and SLIBFP.LIB) in the object code for the linker. All .LIB files are placed in a subdirectory known, with great originality, as \LIB. The emulator is therefore fully specified by

```
\LIB\EM.LIB
```

and the \LIB subdirectory usually resides on the same disk as the \BIN\LINK.EXE and \BIN\LIB.EXE in the case of a floppy disk environment (with the remaining relevant BIB\ files, and the \INCLUDE \INCLUDE\SYS files being on another disk).

Setting up the system

When the compiler (MSC.EXE) is invoked, the compiler determines whether certain 'standard' places have been specified. The designation of these standard places is performed by use of what are termed 'environmental' variables in MSDOS. The MSC.EXE program looks for three environmental variables (PATH INCLUDE TMP), and the LINK.EXE program uses three environmental variables (PATH LIB TMP).

The environmental variables can be set by use of SET and PATH where, for example, using a hard disk (drive C:) three variables can be set by

```
SET INCLUDE=C:\INCLUDE
SET LIB=C:\LIB
SET TMP=C:\
```

That is, whenever the variable INCLUDE is encountered, it is equivalent to the subdirectory \INCLUDE on the hard disk C:, and, for example, the temporary disk area TMP is set equal to the top level directory on the hard disk. The INCLUDE variable asserts the location of the #include files, the LIB variable indicates where to look for library files, and more than one path to a subdirectory can be specified if the paths are separated by semicolons.

The PATH environmental variable differs in that the command is specific:

```
PATH C:\BIN
```

and this variable tells the system where to look for executable files. That is, when the name of an executable file is entered, and the file is not in the current directory, MSDOS looks at the PATH variable to find if there is anywhere else to look (and in this case looks in the C:\BIN directory). More than one path may be specified (separated by semicolons). If floppy disks are being used, a set up recommended by the MC manual is

```
PATH A:\BIN
SET INCLUDE=A:\INCLUDE
SET LIB=A:\LIB
SET TMP=B:\
```

where the compiler is run from drive B:, and the two disks with the C files are swapped in and out of drive A:. Programs are created and stored on the disk in drive B:, which is also the disk used for temporary files. I have made one modification to the suggested format of the PATH command, in that I have added an extra PATH option:

```
PATH C:\BIN;C:\
```

in the case of a hard disk, or

```
PATH A:\BIN;A:\
```

for a standard floppy disk arrangement. Note that there should be no spaces between the semicolon and the next directory designation.

The other aspect to be set up is the operating system configuration, which is performed by use of the MSDOS file known as CONFIG.SYS. The number of files which can be opened at any time (a XENIX-like facility) is set to a minimum of 10, and the number of disk buffers is set to 10 by

```
files = 10
buffers = 10
```

that is, as C makes extensive use of files, the system has to be prepared for all these files.

The best way of setting up the system for the use of C is to use an AUTOEXEC.BAT file, which is a special 'batch' program that comes into operation when the computer is activated. A batch program is the equivalent of a 'shell' program in UNIX, or at least almost equivalent. I have a twin floppy disk system, and as the two program disks (those with MSC.EXE and LINK.EXE) are so full, I have another disk which is used for booting the system. On that disk I have a word processor, to prepare the source program files, as well as a batch file. Thus the disk contains a CONFIG.SYS file, an AUTOEXEC.BAT file, plus associated word processor driver programs (it is to use these programs with ease that I have added another option to the PATH).

The content of the CONFIG.SYS file is

```
buffers=10
files=10
shell=B:command.com /p
```

which sets the buffers to 10, the number of files accessible to 10, and tells MSDOS where to look for the command level interpreter COM-MAND.COM (that is, on drive B: where the situation of the program is independent of the logged drive; /p means 'permanent').

The AUTOEXEC.BAT file is far more interesting:

```
ECHO OFF
CLS
DATE
TIME
PATH A:\BIN;A:\
SET INCLUDE=A:\INCLUDE
SET LIB=A:\LIB
SET TMP=B:\
B:
DIR /W
```

The AUTOEXEC.BAT is automatically activated when the user switches on the computer, and the file contains a sequence of commands. Execution starts by activating an instruction that the ECHOing of commands is turned OFF, then the screen is cleared (CLS), and the user is asked for the DATE and TIME.

When the DATE and TIME commands have been executed and the user has responded, the next commands (with PATH and SET) are those given above to create a standard environment for the operation of MC. The logged disk drive is changed to drive B: (from the boot drive A:), and a directory is produced in Wide format. The directory is that of the data disk, that is, the disk used to create programs (both source code and object code). On the data disk are two special batch programs CRUN.BAT and CCOMP.BAT to be described in the next section but one.

Compiling a program

On one data disk there is a file INTRO.C, whose content is the program:

```
/* INTRO.C */

/* string manipulation example */

/* Boris Allan */


#define INTROC "IntroC"

#include <string.h>

main(argc, argv, envp)

    int argc;
    char **argv, **envp;

    {
        register char **p;

    /* print out the argument list */

        for (p = argv; argc > 0; argc--,p++)
            {
            printf("%s\n", *p);
            if (strcmpi(*p, INTROC) == 0)
                {
                if (strcmp(*p, INTROC) == 0)
                    printf("%s is book title\n",
                            INTROC);
                else
                    printf("%s is true title\n",
                            INTROC);
                }
            }

    /* print out the environment settings   */
    /* which are terminated by a NULL entry */

        printf("\n");
```

```
for (p = envp; *p; p++)
    {
    printf("%s\n", *p);
    }

printf("Final entry is %s\n", *p);

exit(0);

}
```

It is a program partly based on an example called DEMO.C in the Microsoft C documentation, where I have extended the action of the DEMO.C program to use specific MC string comparison functions.

The interpretation of the content of INTRO.C will be left until later, and at the moment we will be concerned with the way in which the source program (INTRO.C) is translated to produce the object code (executable) program INTRO.EXE. The translation is performed in two main stages: compilation, and linking. Compilation is performed by the program MSC.EXE and linking is performed by the program LINK.EXE.

A standard compilation of INTRO.C, that is, to produce an unlinked object code program INTRO.OBJ without any annotated listing, we enter

MSC INTRO;

or

msc intro;

with the disk containing the MSC.EXE file being stored on the disk in drive A:. There is no need to specify the drive and directory for MSC (by A:\BIN\MSC) because the PATH directive instructs MSDOS to search for the program in the directory A:\BIN as well as the current directory.

The outcome of using the MSC compiler program with INTRO.C (note that the .C is assumed, unless otherwise specified) is to produce an object code file INTRO.OBJ. The INTRO.OBJ file can be used for input to the next stage of the process, that is, the linker. The linker assumes an .OBJ file extension and thus to operate the linker the command is

LINK INTRO;

or

link intro;

which automatically links in certain library files stored on the same disk as LINK.EXE (in a directory A:\LIB). Before we can link, therefore, we have to swap the disks in drive A:.

Many options are possible, but for most programs the sequence is simply

```
msc PROG_NAME;

..........

link PROG_NAME;
```

and to run the executable object code program PROG_NAME.EXE we enter

```
PROG_NAME
```

which is an easy sequence to remember. There seems no reason why such a simple sequence should not be automated, and if there is a need for a more adventurous sequence then automation must stop – unless a complicated system is implemented.

Automating compilation

Automation takes place via two batch files CCOMP.BAT and CRUN.BAT which are executed by entering

```
ccomp PROG_NAME
```

or

```
crun PROG_NAME
```

either to compile and link the program PROG_NAME.C or to compile, link and execute the program PROG_NAME.C.

The content of the batch file CCOMP.BAT is

```
echo off
cls
msc %1;
echo
echo PLEASE CHANGE DISKS IN DRIVE A:
pause
echo off
link %1;
```

which turns OFF the ECHO, clears the screen (CLS), and then executes the compiler program MSC.EXE with the name of the source file being %1, followed by a semicolon. The meaning of %1 is that it represents the first parameter to the batch file (for example, PROG_NAME), so 'msc %1;' will be expanded so that the first parameter will be placed next to the semicolon, that is:

```
msc PROG_NAME;
```

This line is thus an injunction to execute MSC.EXE where only the default options are operative (indicated by the ';'). Once the compiler program has finished (a program which actually uses P0.EXE P1.EXE P2.EXE P3.EXE), an instruction 'PLEASE CHANGE DISKS IN DRIVE A:' is output on the screen, and a pause instruction is given – so that the disk can be changed (the system waits for the user to hit a key).

After reasserting that the ECHO is OFF, the LINK.EXE program is executed with the same parameter as MSC, thus the instruction to the system is

```
link PROG_NAME;
```

and the file PROG_NAME.OBJ is automatically linked to the standard libraries EM.LIB SLIBFP.LIB SLIBC.LIB. The sequence then ends with a return to command level, leaving a file PROG_NAME.EXE ready to be executed by entering

```
PROG_NAME
```

At certain times you may wish to add arguments/parameters to the program instruction, but at other times the program needs no arguments and so it can be directly executed. This direct execution is performed by the batch file CRUN.BAT, which has many correspondences with CCOMP.BAT

```
echo off
cls
msc %1;
echo
echo PLEASE CHANGE DISKS IN DRIVE A:
pause
echo off
link %1;
echo off
%1
```

The only difference, in fact, is the addition of the automatic execution of the program, by entering the program (that is, %1).

To compile, link and execute a program, therefore, one enters

```
crun PROG_NAME
```

with a swapping of the disks part way through the sequence.

The action of the program

The program INTRO.C was compiled, linked and executed by

```
crun intro
```

and the output of the program was

```
COMSPEC=\COMMAND.COM
PATH=A:\BIN;A:\
INCLUDE=A:\INCLUDE
LIB=A:\LIB
TMP=B:\
Final entry is (null)
```

The compiled program was then executed a second time, on this occasion adding some arguments after the program name, that is:

```
intro in introc int intr introC intro i introc
        ntroc troc IntroC

/* Note that the above is on one logical line */
```

to which injunction the output of the program was

```
in
introc
IntroC is true title
int
intr
introC
IntroC is true title
intro
i
Introc
IntroC is true title
ntroc
troc
IntroC
IntroC is book title

COMSPEC=\COMMAND.COM
PATH=A:\BIN;A:\
INCLUDE=A:\INCLUDE
LIB=A:\LIB
TMP=B:\
Final entry is (null)
```

The output concerns two main classes of information: the values of the standard MSDOS environment variables (which can be found also by issuing the command SET), and the arguments to the program name. In the INTRO.C program, the main function has three arguments: the first gives the number of arguments in the program command line; the second is a pointer to pointers to characters (that is, a pointer to strings holding the command line arguments), and the third is a pointer to strings containing the environmental variable settings.

Here is the listing of the INTRO.C program repeated:

```
/* INTRO.C */

/* string manipulation example */

/* Boris Allan */


#define INTROC "IntroC"

#include <string.h>

main(argc, argv, envp)

    int argc;
    char **argv, **envp;

    {
        register char **p;

    /* print out the argument list */

        for (p = argv; argc > 0; argc--,p++)
            {
            printf("%s\n", *p);
            if (strcmpi(*p, INTROC) == 0)
                {
                if (strcmp(*p, INTROC) == 0)
                    printf("%s is book title\n",
                            INTROC);
                else
                    printf("%s is true title\n",
                            INTROC);
                }
            }

    /* print out the environment settings   */
    /* which are terminated by a NULL entry */

        printf("\n");
```

```
for (p = envp; *p; p++)
   {
   printf("%s\n", *p);
   }

printf("Final entry is %s\n", *p);

exit(0);

}
```

The content of the program

I will examine the content of this program in sections, where the first section extends from the program heading to the start of the definition of the content of the main() function. That is:

```
#define INTROC "IntroC"

#include <string.h>

main(argc, argv, envp)

   int argc;
   char **argv, **envp;
```

it starts by defining INTROC as being equivalent to the string "IntroC", so that whenever the compiler meets the identifier INTROC, the identifier is replaced by the string "IntroC".

Later in the program we will be using various string manipulation functions and thus the necessary information on the functions is included from the header file <string.h>, where the angle brackets mean that only the 'standard' places on disk are searched. The standard places for #include are the directories given by the environment variable INCLUDE (that is, A:\LIB). If the file was enclosed in double quotes, that is, "string.h" then the search for the file would be started in the current directory, and possibly various other places. The form "string.h" is often used to distinguish a user written header file from the standard library version.

The main() function has certain arguments, that is, 'main(argc, argv, envp)' and the types of the arguments are declared as integer for argc, and a pointer to a pointer to a character for argv and envp. Another way of conceptualising argv and envp is to consider them as pointers to vectors of varying size, or as vectors of vectors of varying size.

Effectively, argv and envp are pointers to the starts of two lists of numbers (val_1) where each val_1 number can be regarded as a pointer. Thus each val_1 number within the list is itself a pointer to the start of another list of numbers (val_2), each of which val_2 numbers is regarded as representing a character. A list of characters is a string, and normally the end of a string is denoted by a NULL value (that is, \0) and when, later in the program, a string is printed, the function knows that the string is ended by checking for the NULL. In fact the #define can be altered to

```
#define INTROC "IntroC\0"
```

without any modification to the program (the string will be ended by two NULLS).

The argc parameter gives the number of arguments in the command line of the calling program; the argv parameter contains a pointer to the start of pointers to the strings containing the names of the arguments in the command line; and the envp parameter contains a pointer to the start of pointers to the strings containing the names of the environmental variables. There is no parameter which gives the number of environmental variables, but we know that the list of variables is terminated by a NULL string.

The definition of the action of the main( ) function commences with the opening **{** and there is a declaration

```
register char **p;
```

a definition of an automatic (local) variable which indicates that p is a pointer to a pointer to a character. The storage of the pointer value is to be in a register (to speed access to values), but such a declaration as register is not particularly necessary.

The first main subsection of the main( ) function is

```
for (p = argv; argc > 0; argc--,p++)
    {
    printf("%s\n", *p);
    if (strcmpi(*p, INTROC) == 0)
        {
        if (strcmp(*p, INTROC) == 0)
            printf("%s is book title\n",
                    INTROC);
        else
            printf("%s is true title\n",
                    INTROC);
        }
    }
```

The three sections of the for loop are

```
(p = argv;
```

```
argc > 0;
```

```
argc--,p++)
```

In the first section the pointer to pointers, p, is set equal to argv so that p points to the start of the argv list of pointers, and in the second section the test is that the number of arguments is greater than zero.

The first action of the for loop is to print out the string (%s) to which p is pointing (followed by a newline, that is, \n). There is then a test to see if the string given by *p is equal to the string defined by INTROC, without regard to case. The case independent test 'strcmpi(*p, INTROC)' produces the value −1 if *p is less (earlier in the alphabet) than INTROC, 0 if the two strings are indentical, and +1 if *p is later in the alphabet than INTROC. If the two strings are identical then the result is zero, and this is why there is a further test '== 0'. If the test is false the next iteration of the loop is commenced.

There are two different cases when *p is the same as INTROC (that is, "IntroC"): the first case is that when the two strings are exactly identical, and the second is when the two strings contain the same letters but the cases differ. The test 'strcmp(*p, INTROC) == 0' checks to see if the strings are identical, and if they are identical we are told the book title, whereas if the parameter and "IntroC" are of different cases then we are told the correct title.

The final section to the loop adds one unit to the p pointer and subtracts one from the number of command line arguments (thus when argc has reached zero, the last argument is output and the loop terminates on the next check of 'argc > 0'). The 'unit' which is added to p is equivalent to the size of a pointer (in bytes).

The next for loop checks the environmental variables, terminating the loop when the string is NULL.

```
printf("\n");

for (p = envp; *p; p++)
    {
    printf("%s\n", *p);
    }

printf("Final entry is %s\n", *p);

exit(0);

}
```

The three sections to the for loop expression are

```
(p = envp;
```

```
*p;
```

```
p++)
```

In the first section p is assigned to the start of the envp list of pointers; the test is whether the string to which p is pointing is NULL (that is, of value \0). The string is printed, and the value of the pointer incremented by one unit, and thus the loop continues until p points to a NULL string. After the loop is over the content of the final (empty) string is printed, with the result that the output is

```
Final entry is (null)
```

The symbol '(null)' is how the NULL string is output by the printf function.

If you check the above output listings and compare the command line arguments with the printed strings and the title information, you will see how INTRO.C operates.

These string comparisons will be of use in the construction of the Varith translator in the next chapter.

Chapter Five
Constructing a Language Translator: Tokens

One of the most frequent uses of C is the construction of systems programs, and one of the key types of systems program for which C is so suited is the construction of language translators.

This suitability is not surprising given C's origins with BCPL (designed as a compiler writer). What is perhaps well worth emphasising is that most complex software packages are, effectively, versions of languages designed for specific purposes. Getting a package to produce results is an exercise in programming, even though the input mechanism may be a pointing device and the medium of communication be via the use of icons.

Obviously, certain packages are more programmable than others, that is, some packages can be instructed to perform a wider range of tasks than others. Database packages of any sophistication, for example, can be programmed to perform more tasks than the designer originally envisaged: in fact, many database systems are termed languages. The point is that the production of software is, in general, the construction of an applications language of some form or other.

It is for this reason that we will see how a very simple programming language is implemented in C, a simple but useful language. The language is to be called Varith. The discussion in this chapter will introduce the necessary groundwork for the operation of the translator, that is, reading in the program lines and isolating the distinct items.

The Varith translator

The idea behind the Varith translator is to produce an interactive system which has certain characteristics of a calculator, but which also has a facility to use variables, where variables can have names composed of any number of characters (starting with a letter). An example of Varith is

```
NEW = (OLD + 3) * 5
```

where, within this one line, we can note certain important characteristics of this language (and most other languages).

1. There are variables in the language (in this case, 'NEW' and 'OLD'), and in general there are two types of variables:
   - Those to which no value has been assigned (and which can only be used on the left-hand side of an assignment); and
   - Those which have an assigned value, and which can appear either side of an assignment.
2. There are constants (in this case, '3' and '5').
3. There are expression delimiters (in this case, '(' and ')') which group elements within the expression on the right-hand side of the assignment.
4. There are operators (in this case, '=' '+' and '*') which act on values produced by variables and constants.

Each of these categories needs to be treated differently so, in effect, there are five classes of object in the language with which we have to deal (we will not implement any functions or procedures). Each of these classes of object will possess a different set of methods which characterise the behaviour of members of that class.

Any object is thus described by two principal characteristics: the object's class, and the object's identifier within that class. Each class of object is described by the set of internal methods which characterise that class, and (in addition) the class defines what can be done to its objects and what objects can do. The purpose of a translator is to take a line such as

```
NEW = (OLD + 3) * 5
```

to decide what are the basic objects, and then ascertain the class which describes each object. Each object has an associated set of methods, so the translator has to establish the necessary methods for each object.

The techniques we use to turn a line of Varith into some form which can be evaluated will be described step by step as we go through the translator, but at this stage the outline sequence is

Reading the source
When a line of instructions is entered at the keyboard we need to be able to read in that line, and store the input in some easily accessible form.

Source into tokens
The line of input is composed of characters, so the first task is to go through the characters, disentangling the relevant tokens such as 'NEW' or ')', without any attempt to interpret the meaning of the tokens. This chapter examines these two stages.

Tokens into objects
When we have the line of input in the form of tokens, we need to go through the input to establish the basic objects in the line, storing the information about the objects in the form of their class and item. Frequently, this is known as the lexical phase.

Objects into order
When the natures of the objects in the input line have been established, the objects have to be resequenced into some order (dependent upon their methods) which is accessible for computer operation. This is termed the parsing stage, and together with the lexical phase is discussed in the next chapter.

Executing the objects
The parsed sequence of objects is then examined, and executed according to the methods which characterise each object. This the execution stage, examined in Chapter 7

Each of the above phases will be treated as a separate entity even though in some translators more than one phase is performed at one time, and in some languages (for example, Pascal) all phases are combined to produce a one pass compiler (though this has dramatic effects on the form of the language). The distinction between the phases will be maintained because

● It is clearer to see how the translator is constructed, and
● It is simpler to program

if each of the phases is kept as a distinct program entity. The translator will, therefore, be composed of the following routines (functions):

1. lineIn
2. makeTokens
3. makeObjects
4. orderObjects
5. execute

with many other subsidiary routines which will be used by these principal routines.

Reading the source

Here is the lineIn( ) routine (written in Microsoft C):

```
/* file lex.h */

/* Boris Allan */


lineIn(buffer)

    char buffer[];
```

```
{
    int counter, chval;

    for (counter = 0;
         counter < (MAXBUFF - 1) &&
         ((chval = getchar()) != EOF) &&
         (chval != '\n');
         counter++)
      buffer[counter] = chval;

    buffer[counter] = '\0';
    fflush(stdin);

}
```

The lineIn() routine is contained in a header file LEX.H, along with other routines for the lexical phase. The routine takes as its argument a variable known as buffer, which is declared as an array of characters (or a string). Two local variables (counter and chval) are defined as integers, and the first is used to count the number of characters that have been read from the standard input channel (stdin), with chval containing the value of the character last read from that channel.

The for loop initialises the counter to zero, and the test is whether the counter is one less than the maximum size of the buffer, or the end of file has been read, or a newline has been encountered. If none of these has happened then the value read (chval) is assigned to the appropriate element of the character array, the counter is incremented by one, and the test is made again. When the loop ends, the final element (that is, one element after the last valid value) is set to the NULL character to specify the end of the string.

Sometimes more characters have been entered than can fit into the buffer, so not all are transferred. It is for this reason that the standard input channel is flushed (that is, emptied of all further characters) by the use of fflush(stdin). This is a precaution against possible contamination.

An example of the use of lineIn() is

```
/* test of lineIn() */

/* Boris Allan */



#include "enVarith.h"

main()

    {
```

```
char inline[MAXBUFF];

do
    {
    lineIn(inline);
    printf("%s\n", inline);
    }
while (strlen(inline) != 0);
printf("%s\n", inline);
}
```

The #include file enVarith.h is a user defined header file which is used to contain all the environmental information needed for Varith to operate. The #include file is stored by MSDOS as ENVARITH.H, and the specification as enVarith.h is purely to emphasise the importance of Varith. Ignore the content of enVarith.h for the moment, and examine the above program.

The array inline is set to contain MAXBUFF characters (it is a string), then the routine lineIn() is used to read in a string from the keyboard. The string is printed out (as a check), and while the string is not empty (the length is not zero) then 'do' the process of reading in and printing (that is, until the the return key is pressed at the beginning of a line). This program is only a test of lineIn() , and has no other utility. Note that the strlen() function is one of those provided as a standard library by Microsoft, and there are many such utilities used later which derive from that library. The string library is of a fairly standard form.

Source into tokens

The next stage is to take the string, and then extract the appropriate tokens from the string. There are three main classes of tokens to be isolated:

Digitstring
These are tokens which can be taken to represent a number (a constant). A digitstring commences with a digit and continues for as long as there are digits, that is, a digitstring ends with a space, an alphabetic character, or non-alphanumeric character.

Alphastring
These are tokens which can be taken to represent variable names. An alphastring commences with a letter (an alphabetic character) and continues for as long as there are alphanumeric characters, that is, an alphastring ends with a space or an alphanumeric character.

Punctstring
These are tokens (one character) which represent punctuation, that is, all characters other than the alphanumeric.

The function makeTokens() takes a string of characters and isolates the tokens in that string.

Pointers to strings

First of all, study the main() function which is used to test the tokenising function:

```
/* Test of makeTokens() */

/* Boris Allan */


#include "enVarith.h"

main()

    {
        char inline[MAXBUFF], *store[MAXBUFF];
        int numToken, counter;

        do
            {
            lineIn(inline);

            numToken = makeTokens(inline,store);

            for (counter = 0;
                  counter <= numToken ;
                  counter++)
                printf("%u %s\n",store[counter],
                        store[counter]);

            printf("\n");
            }
        while (strlen(inline) != 0);
    }
```

This program (main() function) declares two variables which are integer (numToken and counter), an array of MAXBUFF characters (inline), and an array of MAXBUFF pointers to characters (store).

inline stores a list of characters (up to a maximum of MAXBUFF) and is used to read in the line of characters entered at the keyboard. There is a great difference between inline and the other array, store, because store is an array of pointers (that is, unsigned integers) where the pointers are pointers to series of characters (that is, strings).

To print a string we specify a pointer to the start of the string in printf( ), and thus to print the string known as buffer we enter

```
printf("%s\n",inline);
```

However, to print a string using store we have to define a pointer first, and then use that pointer to indicate the string to be printed. store[x] (where x is an admissible unsigned integer) provides a pointer to a string, and thus we enter

```
printf("%s\n", store[x]);
```

To make the xth example of store point to the same string as inline, we have to make the pointer store[x] be the same as the pointer to the string inline:

```
store[x] = inline;
```

Note that we have not equated the strings, in that only the pointers have been equated.

The array of up to MAXBUFF pointers to strings (store) is to contain pointers to the strings which represent the tokens. Thus the first token is printed by

```
printf("%s\n", store[0]);
```

or, using explicit pointer notation

```
printf("%s\n", *store);
```

and the last token is printed by

```
printf("%s\n", store[numToken]);
```

This implies that there are numToken + 1 different tokens, where the number of tokens is returned by the function makeTokens. The pointer array is set to MAXBUFF elements because that is the theoretical maximum for an input buffer of MAXBUFF elements.

The input arguments to makeTokens( ) are two addresses (pointers): the first is a pointer to the start of the input buffer, and the second is a pointer to the start of the array of token pointers. The for loop prints out all the tokens preceded by the address at which that token is stored, that is

```
printf("%u %s\n",store[counter],store[counter]);
```

and the do...while loop iterates until the input buffer is empty. To indicate the form of the output, here is a specimen sequence:

```
1 23 456 7890
3388 1
3390 23
```

```
3393 456
3397 7890

NEW=(OLD+3)*5
3388 NEW
3392 =
3394 (
3396 OLD
3400 +
3402 3
3404 )
3406 *
3408 5

//  ////  / / /////
3388 /
3390 /
3392 /
3394 /
3396 /
3398 /
3400 /
3402 /
3404 /
3406 /
3408 /
3410 /
3412 /
```

This output was produced by three lines of input, where the lines are designed to show different ways in which the tokenising function might need to operate:

```
1 23 456 7890
NEW=(OLD+3)*5
//  ////  / / /////
```

First, the tokeniser needs to accommodate different sizes of tokens (separated by spaces); second, it needs to be able to distinguish between different types of token, where the tokens are not separated by spaces; and third, it needs to be able to ignore multiple spaces, and distinguish between successive punctstring tokens, however arranged.

Note that the beginning of the token strings is always at the same location (that is, 3388) and that the number of locations given over to each string is always one greater than the number of characters in the string.

Tokenising in practice

As the function makeTokens( ) works correctly, here is the listing of the
function:

```
/* file token.h */

/* Boris Allan */



makeTokens(buffer,pc)

  char buffer[], *pc[];

  {
  static char p[2*MAXBUFF];
      int counter = 0, end = strlen(buffer),
          incr = 0, number = 0, numToken = 0;

      if (buffer[0] == '\0') return(-1);
              /* my big boob */

      while ( counter < end )
          {
          while (isspace(buffer[counter])
              || iscntrl(buffer[counter])
              || buffer[counter] < 0)
          counter++;

          if (isdigit(buffer[counter]))
              incr = digitstring(buffer+counter,
                      p+number);

          else if (isalpha(buffer[counter]))
              incr = alphastring(buffer+counter,
                      p+number);

          else if (ispunct(buffer[counter]))
              incr = punctstring(buffer+counter,
                      p+number);

          if (counter < end)
              {
              pc[numToken] = p + number;
```

```
                    number += incr;
                    counter += --incr;
                    numToken++;
                    }
            };

        return(--numToken);
    }

digitstring(buffer,p)

    char buffer[], p[];

    {
        int ctr = 0;

        while (isdigit(buffer[ctr])
            && buffer[ctr] > 0)
            {
            p[ctr] = buffer[ctr];
            ctr++;
            };

        p[ctr] = '\0';

        return(++ctr);
    }


alphastring(buffer,p)

    char buffer[], p[];

    {
        int ctr = 0;

        while (isalnum(buffer[ctr])
            && buffer[ctr] > 0)
            {
            p[ctr] = buffer[ctr];
            ctr++;
            };

        p[ctr] = '\0';
```

```
        return(++ctr);
    }

punctstring(buffer,p)

    char buffer[], p[];

    {
        p[0] = buffer[0];
        p[1] = '\0';

        return(2);
    }
```

The two arguments to makeTokens( ), that is, buffer and pc, are declared as being an array of characters and an array of pointers to characters respectively (which conforms with the types in the main program).

Within the body of the function the variable p is declared to be a static array of 2*MAXBUFF characters (the maximum possible usage of p is twice the size of a normal buffer). p is declared as static to allocate permanently the memory locations needed to contain that information, because (when another function is called) the memory which was p's might be given to other variables, unless the storage of p is static (and thus protected).

The integers counter, incr, number, and numToken, are all initialised to zero, and the integer end is initialized to the length of the string to which the variable buffer is pointing. If the buffer is empty the value −1 is returned to the calling routine (as there cannot be a minus number of tokens, this allows a check for an empty string).

My big mistake was to waste a day (well, a few hours) trying to track down the reason why the program was performing strangely after I had made some alterations. I tracked down the culprit almost by accident; it was:

```
    if (buffer[0] = '\0') return(-1);
```

which meant that '\0' was always assigned to buffer[0] and the value −1 returned to the calling function. A friend (Carl Phillips) suggests using

```
    #define IS ==
```

so that one writes

```
    if (buffer[0] IS '\0') return(-1);
```

which has much to recommend it. Watch out; this is one of the most common errors known to C.

The initial value of counter is zero, and counter is used to pick a way through the buffer string so that if the counter is less than the value known as end, then examination of the string can progress. That is, while the value of the counter variable is less than the value of end, execute the following instructions (that is, those within the **()** braces).

The first part of the following instructions is a tiny routine to remove spaces, control characters or non-standard characters between tokens. While the content of buffer[counter] is a space, or (¦¦) a control character, or (¦¦) a value less than zero, the value of the counter is increased by one unit. As soon as an appropriate non-blank character is discovered, control moves to the next section. A negative value for a character in MC corresponds to a value between 128 and 255 for some other versions of C (that is, an ASCII value of 255 corresponds to a value of −1 in MC, and ASCII 128 corresponds to −128). The checks for type of character are defined in an MC standard library with declarations contained in the file CTYPE.H.

The next section of the function is composed of tests:

```
if (test1)
   action1;
else
   if (test2)
      action2;
   else
      if (test3)
         action3;
```

That is, if test1 is true then perform action1, else then check to see if test2 is true, and if true perform action2, else then check the truth of test3, and if true perform action3. Note the sequence of tests is such that only one may be chosen (or none at all).

The first test is whether the character buffer[counter] is a digit, and (if so) the function digitstring() is called, where the first argument is the address of the character (that is, buffer+counter) and the second argument is the address of the next character in the p string. The function returns a value which is stored in incr: this is the width of the number in characters. The next two tests are for a letter (alphastring()) and for a punctuation symbol (punctstring()): the formats are the same as for digitstring().

The final section of the for loop embodies a check to find if the value of counter has been incremented beyond the end of the string buffer. If we are still within the string boundaries, the pointer stored in pc[num Token] is set equal to the address of p + number (where number is the start of the current token). The value of number is increased by incr, and as the value of incr includes one unit for the char '\0', the value of counter is increased by one less than incr. The current token number (numToken) is increased by one unit.

When the for loop is exited, the value of numToken is one greater than the number of tokens, and the value returned from the function is one unit less than numToken.

All the tokenising functions follow a similar pattern, and thus I will concentrate on alphastring. The two arguments (addresses) are declared as being the addresses of the beginnings of strings (arrays of character). The local (automatic) variable ctr is set to zero, and thus can point to the first element in each string. The first character is a letter (or the function would not be chosen) and, while the characters are letters or digits and greater than 0 in value, the content of the string is copied over from buffer to p with ctr being incremented one unit at a time.

At the end of the loop, the last character of the p string is set equal to the NULL ('\0'), and the value returned by the function is the value of the ctr incremented by one unit. The increment by one unit is necessary to point to the next available location of the p string (the value is returned and stored in incr).

Thus far we have read in data from the keyboard and turned the information into distinct tokens, where each token falls into one of three distinct categories:

- Identifier
- Constant
- Punctuation symbol

In the next chapter we will examine how to turn the items in these categories into members of classes of objects according to specific rules of interpretation (rules of meaning, or semantics).

Chapter Six
Constructing a Language Translator: Objects

We have a set of functions which enable us to take a line of input text and turn the line into distinct elements (the elements we have called tokens). The next stage of the process is take those tokens and turn them into objects within certain specified classes. These objects then have to be arranged in such a way as to be susceptible to computer execution.

Computer execution is the topic of the next chapter: in this chapter we take the tokens produced by the earlier methods, turn the tokens into objects (according to specified classes), and then reorder the objects according to the appropriate method for each object. The first problem is to discern the objects and the associated classes.

Tokens into objects

Earlier we found that the main categories of object were:

1. Variables
    1.1. Assigned
    1.2. Nonassigned
2. Constants
3. Delimiters
4. Operators

Thus there are four main classes of object, with class 1 being divided into two subclasses. The first problem is that of allocating tokens to classes. The allocation can proceed in two stages: first, allocate to three main groups – variables, constants, and others; second, divide variables into assigned and unassigned, and others into delimiters, operators, or illegal symbols. If there is an illegal symbol there should be an error message and the translation should end.

The definitions of the classes are:

Variables   Tokens which start with a letter.

Constants   Tokens which start with a number.
Delimiters   Tokens which are (or).
Operators   Tokens which are = + − * / % ^ or ~.

Arithmetic in Varith is integer, and the meanings of the operators are: assign, add, subtract, multiply, divide, modulus, power, and negate. As the class of any object is given definitively by the first character of the token for that object, the first stage of conversion from tokens to objects needs only to look at the first character of any token.

This characteristic leads us to realise there is one further class of object: that of unrecognised tokens, that is, those tokens which have no defined membership under the above scheme. An example of an unrecognised token is, say, # which has no definition within Varith: it is not variable, constant, delimiter, nor operator. Thus within our translator we have first to isolate such tokens as objects within an error class, and then, when we reorder the objects, we have to indicate an error.

Before we can progress, however, we must establish the structures of the objects within the classes, and the form in which we store the objects after assignment to classes.

Data structures

Here, without further ado, are the structures used in the conversion of tokens to objects:

```
#define IDSIZE 10

struct varObj
    {
    char name[IDSIZE];
    char assgd;
    int varVal;
    };

struct genObj
    {
    char class;
    int item;
    };

struct constObj
    {
    int constVal;
    };
```

```
struct symbolObj
  {
  char name;
  char priority;
  int (*function)();
  };

struct genObj objList[MAXBUFF];

struct varObj varList[MAXBUFF];

struct constObj constList[MAXBUFF/2];

struct symbolObj delimList[2];

struct symbolObj operList[8];
```

The five key structures are the final lines of the above listing:

struct genObj objList[MAXBUFF];
This is an array of structures, with MAXBUFF elements. Each element of
the array is an object of the structural form genObj, where genObj is a
structure composed of two elements:

```
struct genObj
  {
  char class;
  int item;
  };
```

The first element is a character which denotes that object's general class, and
the second element gives that object's item number within that class. There
are MAXBUFF elements because that is the maximum number of possible
objects (at one per character position). This array is used to store details
about objects converted from tokens on any one line, and the array is reused
as each new line is entered and converted.

struct varObj varList[MAXBUFF];
This an array of structures, with MAXBUFF elements. Each element of the
array is an object of the structural form varObj, where the structure varObj
is composed of three elements:

```
struct varObj
  {
  char name[IDSIZE];
  char assgd;
  int varVal;
  };
```

The first element of the structure varObj is a string of IDSIZE characters known by the identifier name, which holds the name of a variable (where the name can be up to IDSIZE $-$ 1 characters). The second element is a 'flag' (that is, a two valued variable which differentiates between two states), and the identifier for the flag is assgd – the flag indicates whether the variable has been initialised. The final element of the structure is an integer which contains the value of that variable (known as varVal). Remember that we are only using integer arithmetic with Varith. There are MAXBUFF elements because it is unlikely that there will be more than that number of variables (the number can easily be altered).

struct constObj constList[MAXBUFF/2];
This is an array of structures, with MAXBUFF/2 elements. Each element of the array is an object of the structural form constObj, where constObj is a structure composed of one element:

```
struct constObj
{
int constVal;
};
```

The one element of the structure is an integer which contains the value of the appropriate integer. Later, we will store constants by reference to their position in the class of constants, and multiple examples of the same constant value will be treated as different constants, each with its own copy of that common value. There are are only MAXBUFF/2 constants because it is impossible to cram (legally) any more constants on a line of input. The array is reused as each new line is entered and converted (that is, the first constant will keep altering in value).

struct symbolObj delimList[2];
This is another array of structures, but with only two elements. Both of the elements are objects of the structural form symbolObj, where symbolObj is a structure composed of three elements:

```
struct symbolObj
{
char name;
char priority;
int (*function)();
};
```

The first element is a one character identifier known as name, the second element is a character which gives the symbol's priority level (on which, more later), and the final element is somewhat more opaque. It has an identifier known as function, which is a pointer to a C function which delivers an integer result (it is worth trying to investigate the way in which that description is constructed from the declaration). The third element will contain the name of a function which defines the methods associated with that object.

struct symbolObj operList[8];
This is an array of structures of the same nature as those of delimList, and there are 8 elements in this array. The structure is symbolObj

```
struct symbolObj
   {
   char name;
   char priority;
   int (*function)();
   };
```

and the only real differences between the use of the symbolObj for operList are the priorities and the functions/methods.

The above data structures are designed to be as general as is reasonable given the constraints of an introductory explanation of C. On the one hand, we do not wish to spend too great a time on the niceties of translators and too little time on C, but (on the other) we need to make a realistic attempt at constructing something practical.

It is very easy to construct desk calculator style language translators if the line of input is presented to the translator in a postfix form and there are no variables (in fact K&R have such an example in their Chapter 4, though they use the term 'Reverse Polish Notation' and not 'postfix'). Varith is closer to a proper translator (by 'proper' I mean more like the C language compiler).

Initialising Varith

The above data structures are used by the following routines

```
(*(funcAddress(funcPointer)))()

   int (*funcPointer)();

   {
   return(funcPointer);
   }


initialize()

/* expanded entries for clarity */
```

```
/* funcAddress() is not necessary */
/* see Appendix 4 */

    {
    delimList[0].name = '(';
    delimList[0].priority = 10;
    delimList[0].function
        = funcAddress(leftParen);

    delimList[1].name = ')';
    delimList[1].priority = 0;
    delimList[1].function
        = funcAddress(rightParen);

    operList[0].name = '=';
    operList[0].priority = 1;
    operList[0].function
        = funcAddress(equalOp);

    operList[1].name = '+';
    operList[1].priority = 2;
    operList[1].function
        = funcAddress(plusOp);

    operList[2].name = '-';
    operList[2].priority = 2;
    operList[2].function
        = funcAddress(minusOp);

    operList[3].name = '*';
    operList[3].priority = 3;
    operList[3].function
        = funcAddress(multOp);

    operList[4].name = '/';
    operList[4].priority = 3;
    operList[4].function
        = funcAddress(divOp);

    operList[5].name = '%';
    operList[5].priority = 3;
    operList[5].function
        = funcAddress(modOp);

    operList[6].name = '^';
```

```
operList[6].priority = 4;
operList[6].function
      = funcAddress(powerOp);

operList[7].name = '~';
operList[7].priority = 5;
operList[7].function
      = funcAddress(negOp);

varPointer = -1;
}
```

These functions give initial values to structures for the delimiters and the operators, where each of the triples defines the name, priority, and active function for that delimiter or operator. Thus, for example, the name of operator 7 is the character '~', its priority is 5, and the associated function is known as negOp. This means that the negator acts before (takes priority over) any other operator, and only the parentheses have a higher priority (see later).

We can perform these initialisations because this is information needed before Varith can operate: the names of the variables and values of constants are as yet unknown. The varPointer has to be initialised (to an impossible value) and thus is set to −1.

Making lists of objects

Assuming we have a tokenised line of input, the next problem is to take that line and turn the tokens into objects: this conversion is performed by the function makeObjects( ).

```
makeObjects(token,numTokens)

char *token[];
int numTokens;

{
int counter = 0;

constPointer = 0;

for (; counter <= numTokens ; counter++)
   {
   if (isdigit(token[counter][0]))
      makeConst(token[counter], counter);
```

```
else if (isalpha(token[counter][0]))
    makeVar(token[counter], counter);
else
    makePunct(token[counter], counter);
};
}
```

The input parameters to the function are, first, an array of pointers to characters (char *token[]) and, second, a count of the number of tokens (numTokens) in the input line.

The local variable counter is set to zero and the constPointer is set to zero, and (whilst counter is less than the numTokens) each successive token is examined to find its class. Each token is isolated as either a constant, variable or an item of punctuation, and the class is established by examination of the first character of the list of characters which form the token (that is, token[counter][0]). At the end of each iteration the value of the counter is increased by 1.

The functions to convert the tokens to objects start with makeConst().

```
makeConst(buffer, ctr)

char buffer[];
int ctr;

{
int conValue = atoi(buffer);

constList[constPointer].constVal
    = conValue;

objList[ctr].class = 'c';
objList[ctr].item = constPointer++;
}
```

The first parameter is an array of characters (a string) and the second parameter is a count of the order of the token (that is, ctr). The string is converted from an alphanumeric string to an integer (atoi()) and the result is stored in the variable conValue.

atoi() is a library function, common to most Cs (and defined in K&R), which converts an alphanumeric string into the corresponding integer, with error checks. The conversion is needed because we have, thus far, only been interested in characters and arrays of characters (that is, strings) but it is at this point that we convert from our 'picture' of the number to the number as a numerical value.

The numerical value is stored in the constVal element of the constList[constPointer] structure, where constPointer indicates the next constant value in order, and this position is occupied. This means that the order in which the constants are stored is exactly the order in which the constants are encountered in the input line.

The objects are stored by the objList[] structure, and if the character 'c' is placed in the element class, then this indicates that the object is a constant, and the element known as item contains the order of the constant in the list (constPointer). The order (constPointer) is incremented by one unit, after the assignment (that is constPointer++).

The sequence for establishing items of the object class known as variables is more complex than that used for the constants object class.

```
makeVar(buffer, ctr)

    char buffer[];
    int ctr;

    {
    int varNum = -1, varPlace = 0;

    if (strlen(buffer) > IDSIZE - 1)
       buffer[IDSIZE - 1] = '\0';

    while (varPlace <= varPointer
         && varNum == -1)
       {
       if (strcmp(buffer,varList[varPlace].name)
            == 0)
          {
          varNum = varPlace;
          varPlace = varPointer;
          }
       varPlace++;
       };

    if (varNum == -1)
       {
       varPointer = (varNum = varPlace);
       strcpy(varList[varPointer].name, buffer);
       varList[varPointer].assgd = '\0';
       };

    objList[ctr].class = 'v';
    objList[ctr].item = varNum;
    }
```

The two arguments to the function are: first, the name stored in a character string, buffer[] (commencing with a letter); and second, the position of the variable in the series of input tokens, ctr. At the outset there are no variables, thus we add new variables to an empty list (varList). As further lines of input are tokenised and turned into the appropriate objects, we have to check the varList to see if a variable has already been declared before we add that variable name to varList.

The initial task (after setting the varNum to -1 and the varPlace to 0) is to restrict the size of the name of the variable to IDSIZE $-$ 1 characters by inserting an end of string marker ('\0') at the IDSIZE element of buffer[], which (because the first element is buffer[0]) is buffer[IDSIZE $-$ 1]. The search through the varList is performed while the varPlace is less than the varPointer (where varPointer gives the end of the list), and while the varNum is equal to -1.

If (within the loop) the name and the buffer string are the same when the buffer string is compared with the name at the present element of the varList, then the varNum is set to the corresponding value (given by varPlace), and varPlace is set equal to the end of the list. In any case the value of varPlace is incremented by one unit.

When the loop has been left, there are two possiblities: either varNum is still equal to -1 (and therefore no match has been found), or varNum has a value of 0 or greater (and therefore a match has been found). If no match has been found (that is, varNum is equal to -1), then the varNum is set equal to the final value of varPlace (one greater than the number of present variables), and this value is also assigned to varPointer. The name of the new variable is copied from the buffer, and the assignment status of that variable is set to null.

The final part of the function assigns the class 'v' to the objList, together with the item number within that class (that is, varNum).

The final function takes other characters accepted by the tokenising process, and uses a multiway switch to decide upon class of object and item number (note that the final default category is the class of 'e' – error – objects, that is not having any known function). It would be simple to extend the operators by adding extra cases to the switch, with extra definitions of functions.

```
makePunct(buffer, ctr)

char buffer[];
int ctr;

{
char chval = buffer[0];

switch (chval)
```

```
{
case '(' :
   objList[ctr].class = 'd';
   objList[ctr].item = 0;
   break;

case ')' :
   objList[ctr].class = 'd';
   objList[ctr].item = 1;
   break;

case '=' :
   objList[ctr].class = 'o';
   objList[ctr].item = 0;
   break;

case '+' :
   objList[ctr].class = 'o';
   objList[ctr].item = 1;
   break;

case '-' :
   objList[ctr].class = 'o';
   objList[ctr].item = 2;
   break;

case '*' :
   objList[ctr].class = 'o';
   objList[ctr].item = 3;
   break;

case '/' :
   objList[ctr].class = 'o';
   objList[ctr].item = 4;
   break;

case '%' :
   objList[ctr].class = 'o';
   objList[ctr].item = 5;
   break;

case '^' :
   objList[ctr].class = 'o';
   objList[ctr].item = 6;
   break;
```

```
case '~' :
    objList[ctr].class = 'o';
    objList[ctr].item = 7;
    break;

default :
    objList[ctr].class = 'e';
    objList[ctr].item = 0;
    break;
};
}
```

Using the object functions

A check on the workings of the above functions is provided by the next program:

```
/* test of makeObjects() */

/* Boris Allan */


#include "enVarith.h"

#include "objtypes.h"

main()

    {
    char inline[MAXBUFF], *store[MAXBUFF];
    int numToken, counter;

    initialize();

    while (lineIn(inline),
         printf("%s\n", inline),
         strlen(inline) != 0)
        {

        numToken = makeTokens(inline,store);

        makeObjects(store,numToken);

        for (counter = 0;
```

```
                    counter <= numToken ;
                    counter++)
                printf("%s => %c %d %s\n",
                       store[counter],
                       objList[counter].class,
                       objList[counter].item);

        };
    }
```

Note that the new functions are stored on the file objTypes.h. It is possible to compile each file separately (using extern declarations), but I find that, for a small system such as this, it is simpler to recompile all the source at each trial of the program because I can use my standard batch programs crun and ccomp.

The main() function simply reads in a line, makes tokens, and turns the tokens into objects, leaving the objects in the array objList[]. The contents of the objList are printed out in the form

TOKEN => CLASS ITEM

Below is a sequence of lines of input being turned into objects.

```
a=4        /* INPUT LINE */

a => v 0
= => o 0
4 => c 0


b = a*a +2*(2+2)        /* INPUT LINE */

b => v 1
= => o 0
a => v 0
* => o 3
a => v 0
+ => o 1
2 => c 0
* => o 3
( => d 0
2 => c 1
+ => o 1
2 => c 2
) => d 1


ccccccccccccccccccccc = y/7        /* INPUT LINE */
```

```
ccccccccc => v 2
= => o 0
y => v 3
/ => o 4
7 => c 0


a==cccccccccccccccccccccccccccccccccccccccc%cc21^21cc
        /* INPUT LINE */

a => v 0
= => o 0
= => o 0
ccccccccc => v 2
% => o 5
cc21 => v 4
^ => o 6
21 => c 0
cc => v 5

b&&b&B          /* INPUT LINE */

b => v 1
& => e 0
& => e 0
b => v 1
& => e 0
B => v 6

@2@@2@2@2@2@2@        /* INPUT LINE */

@ => e 0
2 => c 0
@ => e 0
@ => e 0
2 => c 1
@ => e 0
2 => c 2
@ => e 0
2 => c 3
@ => e 0
2 => c 4
@ => e 0
2 => c 5
@ => e 0
```

```
!@#$%^&*()_+-=        /* INPUT LINE */

!  => e 0
@  => e 0
#  => e 0
$  => e 0
%  => o 5
^  => o 6
&  => e 0
*  => o 3
(  => d 0
)  => d 1
_  => e 0
+  => o 1
-  => o 2
=  => o 0
```

The way to study the output is to compare the / * INPUT LINE * / (which does not include the comment, as this has been added later) with the tokens (extreme left), and with the object class for that token and its item number (to the right of the arrow). Note that variable a is v 0 throughout the sequence, and that variable b is v 1 throughout (and so on); note that in the line @2@@2@2@2@2@ each constant value 2 is treated as a separate case; and note that in the last line ! @ # $ % ^ & * ( )_+ - = some symbols are treated as operators and some are given as errors.

The question is how to take that objList and turn it into a sequence suitable for computer analysis. To achieve this we need to reorder the objList to produce a list in which the order is given by a reverse Polish form, that is, produce rpnList.

Reverse Polish conversion

Computers like to perform their operations in sequence, or – if the sequence has to be disrupted – at least in some regular manner. If a translator meets the assignment

```
a = 4 * 3
```

then to implement the assignment the sequence will have to be altered to

```
a 4 3 * =
```

That is, take the variable a, then the numbers 4 and 3, multiply the last two numbers together (to produce 12) and assign the last value to the variable a. The process may be modelled by

INPUT	rpnList	opStack
a = 4 * 3		
= 4 * 3	a	
4 * 3	a	=
* 3	a 4	=
3	a 4	= *
	a 4 3	= *
	a 4 3 *	=
	a 4 3 * =	

Here are three slightly more complex examples:

INPUT	rpnList	opStack
(2 + 3) * (4 + 5/6)		
2 + 3) * (4 + 5/6)		(
+ 3) * (4 + 5/6)	2	(
3) * (4 + 5/6)	2	(+
) * (4 + 5/6)	2 3	(+
* (4 + 5/6)	2 3	(+)
* (4 + 5/6)	2 3 *	
(4 + 5/6)	2 3 *	*
4 + 5/6)	2 3 *	* (
+ 5/6)	2 3 * 4	* (
5/6)	2 3 * 4	* (+
/6)	2 3 * 4 5	* (+
6)	2 3 * 4 5	* (+ /
)	2 3 * 4 5 6	* (+ /
	2 3 * 4 5 6	* (+ /)
	2 3 * 4 5 6 /	* (+
	2 3 * 4 5 6 / +	*
	2 3 * 4 5 6 / + *	

INPUT	rpnList	opStack
4/5 + 6		
/5 + 6	4	
5 + 6	4	/
+ 6	4 5	/
6 (HOLD +)	4 5	/
6	4 5 /	+
	4 5 / 6	+
	4 5 / 6 +	

(1 * (2 + 3))

```
1 * (2 + 3))                                      (
* (2 + 3))           1                            (
(2 + 3))             1                            ( *
2 + 3))              1                            ( * (
+ 3))                1 2                          ( * (
3))                  1 2                          ( * ( +
))                   1 2 3                        ( * ( +
)                    1 2 3                        ( * ( + )
)                    1 2 3 +                      ( *
                     1 2 3 +                      ( * )
                     1 2 3 + *
```

The rpnList is that used by the language translator in the evaluation of an expression, and it is a list of objects in this form that K&R use in the production of their 'calculator' program. The opStack is a temporary data structure onto which operators and delimiters are shunted during the elaboration of the expression.

The above technique is called the shunting algorithm, and takes as its model a train engine pulling trucks from one siding (INPUT) and rearranging them on another siding (rpnList). The driver decides on which siding to leave the truck (either rpnList or opStack) according to a fixed set of rules.

- If the truck in the INPUT siding contains an operand (a constant or variable) then that truck is taken to the rpnList siding without further ado.
- If the truck contains an operator, then the priority level of the operator is compared with that of the last truck in the opStack siding:
  - If the priority of the operator in INPUT is greater than or equal to that in opStack, then the truck is carried across to opStack.
  - If the priority of the operator in INPUT is less than that of the operator in opStack, then the truck in INPUT is held whilst the truck from opStack is carried across to rpnList; the truck on hold is then carried across to opStack.
- If the INPUT truck contains a delimiter:
  - If the delimiter is a left parenthesis, then the truck is taken across to opStack.
  - If the delimiter is a right parenthesis, then the truck is taken to a null siding, all the trucks from the opStack siding are carried across to rpnList until a left parenthesis truck is encountered, when it is taken to the null siding.
- If there are no more trucks in INPUT, then all the trucks from opStack are carried across to the rpnList siding.

This algorithm can be converted from trains to C quite easily. (The following is not a program, rather it is an algorithm written in C.)

```
for (rpnCtr = 0, opCtr = 0, i = 0;
     i <= numTokens; i++)
  {
  typ = objList[i].class ;

  switch (typ)
     {
     case 'e':
        printf("\nInvalid symbol ");
        printf("at item %d\n",i);
        return(-1);
        break;
        case 'c':

     case 'v':
        rpnList[rpnCtr].class = typ;
        rpnList[rpnCtr].item = objList[i].item;
        rpnCtr++;
        break;

     case 'd':
        if (objList[i].item == 0)
           {
           opCtr++;
           opStack[opCtr].class = 'd';
           opStack[opCtr].item = 0;
           }
        else
           {
           while (opStack[opCtr].class != 'd')
              {
              if (opCtr < 1)
                 {
                 printf("\nUnmatched ");
                 printf("right bracket\n");
                 return(-1);
                 };
              rpnList[rpnCtr].class
                 = opStack[opCtr].class;
              rpnList[rpnCtr].item
                 = opStack[opCtr].item;
              opCtr--;
              rpnCtr++;
              };
           opCtr--;
```

```
                      };
                      break;

              case 'o':
                 opCtr++;
                 for (objPrec =
                         operList[objList[i].item].
                            priority;
                       opPrec =
                          operList[opStack[opCtr-1].
                            item].priority,
                       objPrec < opPrec && opCtr > 0;
                       opCtr--, rpnCtr++)
                       {
                       rpnList[rpnCtr].class = 'o';
                       rpnList[rpnCtr].item
                          = opStack[opCtr-1].item;
                       };
                 opStack[opCtr].class = 'o';
                 opStack[opCtr].item
                    = objList[i].item;
                 break;
            };
      };
```

There are quite a few identifiers in this segment which will need to be
defined, and there is a need also for a final section to unpack the opStack
and move its contents over to the rpnList.

The first section, therefore, contains declarations and initialisations:

```
struct genObj rpnList[MAXBUFF];

rpnMake(numTokens)

    int numTokens;

    {
    char typ;
    int rpnCtr, opCtr, i, opPrec, objPrec;
    static struct genObj opStack[MAXBUFF/2];

    opStack[0].class = 'd';
    opStack[0].item = 0;
```

where the most important item to note is that the opStack is local to the
function rpnMake, but it is a static variable, to improve efficiency. The

rpnList is made into a global variable. Both data structures are of the genObj form (that is, class identifier and item identifier).

The algorithmic section of code follows on immediately from the declarations (incidentally, to save confusion, all code for Varith is repeated in Appendix D). After the algorithmic code is:

```
for (; opCtr > 0; opCtr--)
    {
    if (opStack[opCtr].class == 'd')
        {
        printf("\nUnmatched left bracket\n");
        return(-1);
        }
    else
        {
        rpnList[rpnCtr].class = 'o';
        rpnList[rpnCtr].item
            = opStack[opCtr].item;
        rpnCtr++;
        };
    };
rpnCtr--;
return(rpnCtr);
}
```

The rpnMake() function returns the number of different elements in the rpnList, and if −1 is returned there has been an error. This code is collected and saved in a file rpnConv.h, which is used by the following test program.

Testing RPN conversion

The format of the test program closely follows that of previous test programs:

```
/* test of rpnMake() */

/* Boris Allan */


#include "enVarith.h"

#include "objTypes.h"

#include "rpnConv.h"
```

```
main()

    {
        char inline[MAXBUFF], *store[MAXBUFF];
        int numToken, counter;

        initialize();

        while (lineIn(inline),
              printf("\n /* INPUT LINE */\n%s\n\n",
                  inline),
              strlen(inline) != 0)
            {

            numToken = makeTokens(inline,store);

            makeObjects(store,numToken);

            numToken = rpnMake(numToken);

            for (counter = 0;
                 counter <= numToken ;
                 counter++)
                printf("%c   %d\n",
                      rpnList[counter].class,
                      rpnList[counter].item);

            };
    }
```

To see how the program works, here is specimen output from an actual run.
When examining this output note the way in which I have tried to build up a
consistent pattern of examples, so that it is possible to see how the rpnList
storage is implemented.

```
    /* INPUT LINE */
    0+1

    c   0
    c   1
    o   1


    /* INPUT LINE */
    0+1*2+3
```

```
c   0
c   1
c   2
o   3
c   3
o   1
o   1
```

```
 /* INPUT LINE */
(0+1)*2+3
```

```
c   0
c   1
o   1
c   2
o   3
c   3
o   1
```

```
 /* INPUT LINE */
0+1*(2+3)
```

```
c   0
c   1
c   2
c   3
o   1
o   3
o   1
```

```
 /* INPUT LINE */
(0+1)*(2+3)
```

```
c   0
c   1
o   1
c   2
c   3
o   1
o   3
```

```
 /* INPUT LINE */
((0+1)*(2+3)+4)
```

```
c   0
```

```
c   1
o   1
c   2
c   3
o   1
o   3
c   4
o   1
```

```
 /* INPUT LINE */
((0+1)*(2+3)+4)*5
```

```
c   0
c   1
o   1
c   2
c   3
o   1
o   3
c   4
o   1
c   5
o   3
```

```
 /* INPUT LINE */
1+2)
```

```
Unmatched right bracket
```

```
 /* INPUT LINE */
(1+2
```

```
Unmatched left bracket
```

```
 /* INPUT LINE */
!+@
```

```
Invalid symbol at item 0
```

If you study the rpnMake() function it is possible to see how the error messages operate. Note that in the test program there is the assignment 'numToken= rpnMake(numToken);' and numToken is used to determine how many elements are in the rpnList. If the value of the rpnMake( ) function is −1 (an error) nothing is output.

In the final chapter about this interpreter, rpnList is used to perform our calculations.

Chapter Seven
Constructing a Language Translator: Execution

With the data structure rpnList we have available a sequence of objects which completely identify the order of execution for a line of Varith. By means of the other structure varList, we have a record of current values of variables, plus a flag to indicate whether a value has been assigned to a particular variable.

All that we have to perform in this chapter is:

- Decide on how we want Varith to behave in various circumstances, assuming correct input.
- Decide on how the various operators are to be implemented, assuming correct input.
- Decide on how we are going to treat errors in execution (for example, the use of unassigned variables).

The model of execution I wish to use is partially based on the model implicit in C, and thus we can perhaps understand a bit more about C through investigating Varith.

Varith characteristics

Suppose we enter

    3*4

to which we require the response

    => 12

and then we enter

    3*4 5*6

to which the response is

    => 12 30

– the two numbers are output in order. Now progress slightly further, and investigate

    a = 3*4
    => 12

so that the last value used in the input line is still echoed. This implies that any expression ($3*4$ or a $= 3*4$) produces a value, and in this Varith is like C. The desire to add separate short expressions to the list on the stack requires an alteration to the function rpnMake(), in that the action for constants and variables has to be changed:

```
case 'c':
case 'v':
    rpnList[rpnCtr].class = typ;
    rpnList[rpnCtr].item = objList[i].item;
    rpnCtr++;
    if (objList[i+1].class == 'c'
         || objList[i+1].class == 'v')
        {
        for (; opCtr > 0; opCtr--)
            {
            if (opStack[opCtr].class == 'd')
                {
                printf("\nUnmatched left bracket\n");
                return(-1);
                }
            else
                {
                rpnList[rpnCtr].class = 'o';
                rpnList[rpnCtr].item
                    = opStack[opCtr].item;
                rpnCtr++;
                };
            };
        };
    break;
```

Note that there is an extra check, to see if the next object is either a variable or a constant, and if the next object is in fact not an operator or delimiter, then the operators on opStack are unpacked.

One consequence of the property that any expression provides a result, is that multiple assignments such as

```
a = 2*(b = 3*4)
=> 24
a
=> 24
b
=> 12
```

become possible. Another way of printing out the values of a and b is

```
a b
=> 24 12
```

because whatever is left on the stack is printed out at the end of every evaluation.

This requires the use of a stack for values, which I shall term the valStack, where the valStack has to have certain specific characteristics.

1. There has to be an element which distinguishes between constant and variable.
2. If the value is that of a variable, then the item number for the class has to be specified (this allows a check for assigned/unassigned values).
3. If a value has been assigned (variable and constant) then that value should be provided as the third element.

The basic structure of the valStack is thus

```
struct valObj
    {
    char class;
    int item;
    int value;
    };

struct valObj valStack[MAXBUFF/2];
```

At the end of the evaluation of a line, the system merely steps through the stack from valStack[0] to the maximum of the items left on the stack (the reverse of the normal order).

Implementing operators

Each element of the operList has associated with it a pointer to a function (that is, int (*function)( ); – a pointer to a function which delivers an integer result).

If there are no problems with incorrect input, then each function will operate by examining the appropriate number of values at the 'top' of valStack, but unfortunately we have to have a check at this stage. If topStack indicates the current latest value of valStack, then negOp( ), for example, will take the form

```
negOp()
    {
    int varItem;
```

```
if (topStack < 0)
    {
    printf("Too few items on stack\n");
    return(-1);
    }

switch (valStack[topStack].class)
    {
    case 'v':
        varItem = valStack[topStack].item;
        if (varList[varItem].assgd == '\0')
            {
            printf("Unassigned variable\n");
            return(-1);
            };

    case 'c':
        valStack[topStack].value
            = -valStack[topStack].value;
        valStack[topStack].class = 'c';
        return(0);
    };
}
```

This function simply changes the sign of the value on the top of the stack, as long as the value is that of a constant or an assigned variable (note the ripple through in the cases). After changing the sign of the value the class of the object is changed to that of a constant.

Most of the other functions follow a similar pattern to plusOp( )

```
plusOp()
    {
    int leftVal, rightVal;

    if (checkVals() == -1) return(-1);

    rightVal = popStack();
    leftVal = popStack();
    pushStack(leftVal + rightVal);

    return(0);
    }
```

It also has two other useful functions:

```
popStack()
    {
    return(valStack[topStack--].value);
    }

pushStack(pushVal)
    int pushVal;
    {
    topStack++;
    valStack[topStack].value = pushVal;
    valStack[topStack].class = 'c';
    valStack[topStack].item = 0;
    }
```

The popStack() function 'removes' the top item from valStack, with the additional effect that the value of topStack is decreased by one unit, and the value on the top of the stack is returned as the value of the function. The pushStack() function adds the value given as the argument to the function, the class is set to constant, and the item is set to 0.

Activating functions

To activate the appropriate functions, therefore, we have to construct a special function which enables us to act on the pointer to a function:

```
activate(funcPtr)

    int (*funcPtr)();
    {
    return((*funcPtr)());
    }
```

The function pointer is provided as part of the operList data structure. The activate() function is used by the execRpn() function which takes the objects from the rpnList and either stores them on the valStack or (if an operator) activates the appropriate function.

activate() works by accepting an argument which is a pointer to a function delivering an integer result, and (*funcPtr)() activates the function which is associated with that pointer. The form of the execRpn() function is that, if the next object in the rpnList is a constant or a variable, this information is transferred. If the next object is an operator then the function is activated.

```
execRpn(numTokens)

    int numTokens;
    {
    static int ctr;
    ctr = 0;
    topStack = -1;

    while (ctr <= numTokens)
        {
        switch (rpnList[ctr].class)
            {
            case 'c':
                topStack++;
                valStack[topStack].class = 'c';
                valStack[topStack].item = 0;
                valStack[topStack].value
                    = constList[rpnList[ctr].item].
                            constVal;
                break;

            case 'v':
                topStack++;
                valStack[topStack].class = 'v';
                valStack[topStack].item
                    = rpnList[ctr].item;
                valStack[topStack].value
                    = varList[rpnList[ctr].item].
                            varVal;
                break;

            case 'o':
                if (activate(operList[rpnList[ctr].
                        item].function)
                    == -1)
                    return(-1);
                break;
            };
        ctr++;
        };
    return(topStack);
}
```

The execRpn( ) function returns the number of items left on the stack (that is, the last value of topStack, which is – in fact – one less than the number of elements). The complete listing of all the required functions is given in Appendix D, but one particularly interesting function is that for the assignment of a value to variable:

```
equalOp()
   {
   int varItem, tempVal;

   if (topStack < 1)
      {
      printf("Too few items on stack\n");
      return(-1);
      }

   if (valStack[topStack-1].class == 'c')
      {
      printf("Assignment to constant\n");
      return(-1);
      }

   varItem = valStack[topStack].item;

   if (valStack[topStack].class == 'v'
         && varList[varItem].assgd == '\0')
      {
      printf("Unassigned variable\n");
      return(-1);
      };

   tempVal = popStack();
   valStack[topStack].class = 'c';
   valStack[topStack].value = tempVal;
   varItem = valStack[topStack].item;
   varList[varItem].varVal = tempVal;
   varList[varItem].assgd = '\1';

   return(0);
   }
```

I will examine the function in segments because each has a distinct purpose.

```
equalOp()
   {
   int varItem, tempVal;

   if (topStack < 1)
```

```
{
printf("Too few items on stack\n");
return(-1);
}
```

This is a check to establish that there are sufficient objects already on the stack; there have to be at least two objects (topStack must be at least 1). The error return is the normal −1, a value which is checked in execRpn() by means of the expression

```
activate(operList[rpnList[ctr].item].function) == -1)
```

This expression means that the function to which operList[rpnList[ctr].item].function is pointing is executed before the check is made. The next attempt to diagnose errors is

```
if (valStack[topStack-1].class == 'c')
    {
    printf("Assignment to constant\n");
    return(-1);
    }
```

The object earlier on the valStack (that is, at topStack−1) has to be a variable for any legal assignment to be performed, and this is the purpose of the check.

It is impossible to assign to a constant, and it is also impossible to assign from a variable which has no value:

```
varItem = valStack[topStack].item;

if (valStack[topStack].class == 'v'
        && varList[varItem].assgd == '\0')
    {
    printf("Unassigned variable\n");
    return(-1);
    };
```

This is the end of the special checks: the main assignment of a value is performed by

```
tempVal = popStack();
valStack[topStack].class = 'c';
valStack[topStack].value = tempVal;
varItem = valStack[topStack].item;
varList[varItem].varVal = tempVal;
varList[varItem].assgd = '\1';

return(0);
```

This sequence pops the top value off the stack and stores the value in tempVal, sets the nature of the object which is to receive the value to constant class, assigns the tempVal to that object, and (after finding the approriate varItem) assigns both a value and an 'assigned' status to that variable. The function ends with the return of a zero value.

Running Varith

The driver program for Varith is

```
/* test of Varith */

/* Boris Allan */


#include "enVarith.h"

#include "objTypes.h"

#include "rpnConv.h"

#include "exec.h"

main()

    {

    char inline[MAXBUFF], *store[MAXBUFF];
    int numToken, counter;

    initialize();

    while (lineIn(inline),
        strlen(inline) != 0)
        {

        numToken = makeTokens(inline,store);

        makeObjects(store,numToken);

        numToken = rpnMake(numToken);

        numToken = execRpn(numToken);

        printf("=> ");
```

```
for (counter = 0;
        counter <= numToken ;
        counter++)
    printf("%d ",
           valStack[counter].value);
printf("\n");

    };
}
```

I have kept the pattern of this driver program similar to those given previously so that its structure can be followed with less effort.

The performance of the program is perhaps best studied by means of a few examples:

```
2*3

=> 6

a=2*3+1

=> 7

b=3*(c=a*a)

=> 147

a b c

=> 7 147 49

1+2)


Unmatched right bracket
=>

!+2


Invalid symbol at item 0
=>

(1+2


Unmatched left bracket
=>
```

What we have produced, therefore, is a useful system which is a stand alone program occupying about 10K of compiled code.

Getting this system to work will help you understand how the various aspects of C tie together: it is probably true to say that the key to the constructive use of C is the structure.

In the final chapter we will look briefly at three different ways of using C, more as examples of what might be accomplished than as definitive statements of how C should or should not be.

Chapter Eight
Prospects

Before we move on to discuss newer approaches it might be worth using Varith to examine integer arithmetic in C. The reason why it is so interesting is that integer arithmetic shows with great clarity characteristics of C which are of more general applicability. An important point to remember is that C, though officially typed, is effectively an untyped language in that checks on bounds are absent, and any C data item can be used for purposes other than those which might be intended.

Aspects of flexibility

A clear example is the char data type, which does not store characters as such, merely their ASCII equivalent values. Most computer languages store characters as ASCII equivalents, but perform an automatic conversion from the value to the character when the variable is used. C always uses the ASCII values for characters, and to convert from the ASCII value always requires some coercion: for example, the check

```
if (charVal == '\0')
```

equates the value of charVal with the ASCII equivalent of the character '\0', and

```
printf("%c\n", charVal);
```

means that the value of charVal is turned into its character equivalent for output.

A further aspect well worth remembering is that if an array has ten elements (with indices ranging from 0 to 9), then it's possible to access an element with the index −1 (say), or with the index 10 (say). As accessing array elements is performed by the simple addition of a multiple of the appropriate size of value to a base address, then silly accesses are possible. The bonus one gets from lack of such checks is speed of execution (as FORTH has discovered also, checks take time), but the penalty is insecurity (as we can see by using Varith).

Here is a Varith dialogue:

```
32767+32767
=> -2
32767*2
=> -2
32768 16384*2
=> -32768 -32768
b=2*(a=16384*2)
=> 0
a b
=> -32768 0
2^14 2^15 2^16
=> 16384 -32768 0
256*256
=> 0
```

All the above strange results become immediately comprehensible if we realise that the version of C in which Varith is implemented (that is, Microsoft C) stores integers in two bytes (sixteen bits) using complement arithmetic. The range of values for integers is thus −32768 to 32767 with the value 32768 being understood by C as −32768 and the value 65535 being understood as −1.

There are no checks to stop 'sillinesses' such as 16384*2 being regarded as −32768, but then you can use such facilities to effect if you are knowledgeable. C is not a language for the unaware.

Structures and objects

The design philosophy which informed Varith can be termed an 'object oriented' methodology, in that the basic problem was seen in terms of trying to establish key classes of objects which made the solution of the problem more comprehensible.

Any object was a member of a class, and each class had an associated set of methods which characterised that class. A distinction was made between tokens, the labels used to describe the elements (the names), and objects, which had a structure and associated methods. An object class was (in fact) a data structure type, and in using an object oriented methodology one is forced into frequent use of data structures. Most C programmers make extensive use of data structures, and many use (unwittingly) a variant of the object oriented methodology because such a methodology is a natural way of thinking about any complex situation.

Though I used data structures a great deal in the production of Varith, the nature of the topic was such that structures were either global or local to functions. There was no need to pass structures as arguments to functions. It

is for that reason that there were no pointers to structures using the →
selection arrow, but one object oriented approach to C makes extensive use
of such pointers.

Known as Objective-C, this system has a special preprocessor which sets
up special types of data structures and methods to emulate part of the
techniques available in the language Smalltalk-80. Consider the task of
printing out a value (where the value may be the complex value of a
structure): at each use of print we need to specify the nature of the structure
for which we require the value. At the simplest level, when using printf( ) we
need to specify the type of the object to be printed, for example %d or %s.

It is possible to design languages (for example, Algol 68) which can
extend the definition of any operator or function to accommodate new uses
of that operator or function. The problem with this technique is that strong
type checking is needed (difficult to implement in C), and a language has to
provide what is termed 'static' binding (any extension to the language types
has to be explicitly developed).

Static binding means that, for example, whenever a new type is
introduced, a new definition of each function or operator has to be
produced. With such an approach, the development of extensions to the
system means extensive rewriting of code. The problem comes from what is
termed the operator/operand syndrome: the operator (the doer of the
action) has to decide how to operate on that operand. In an object
oriented approach the object decides how the action (the message) is to
be implemented, by looking at the methods associated with that object.

Smalltalk is expensive in terms of machine resources though Smalltalk
programs tend to be far shorter than programs in many other languages,
partly because the flexibility of the object oriented approach eats up such
resources. The *Objective-C Sample Reference Manual* (from Productivity
Products International) says:

> Smalltalk-80 is hard on machine resources – almost *orders of*
> *magnitude* in performance have evaporated in providing automatic
> garbage collection, the interactive environment, and the graphical user
> interface. Although this may be reasonable in an environment for
> software researchers, many companies and the market which buys their
> products are just not prepared to pay such a price regardless of the cost
> and scarcity of high quality programmers.

Objective-C provides a new layer of superstructure to the existing C
structures. This new superstructure adds classes, objects, messages, and the
notion of inheritance, where inheritance is the ability to produce subclasses
which carry over (inherit) methods and characteristics of the originating
class of which they are subclasses.

Objective-C is such a novel (and useful) superstructure to C – existing C
facilities are unaffected – that such extensions are well worth pursuing. Here

is an example of the object oriented methodology taken from the Objective-C manual:

```
extern id Container, Pen, Pencil,
        LetterOpener, Scissors;

id pencilCup = [Container new];

[pencilCup add: [Pen blue]];
[pencilCup add: [Pen red]];
[pencilCup add: [Pen green]];
[pencilCup add: [Pencil new]];
[pencilcup add: [LetterOpener]];
[pencilcup add: [Scissors new]];
```

The identifiers Container, Pen, Pencil, LetterOpener and Scissors are classes of objects defined externally to the present file, of type id. The new type known as id is defined as being equivalent to a pointer to a special type _PRIVATE by the declaration

```
typedef struct _PRIVATE *id;
```

which is automatically generated at the beginning of every compiled file.

There is a declaration and initialisation of an object pencilCup, which is a new instance of the Container class. The type of pencilCup is the same as that of the classes, because a class is also an object and what defines the nature of pencilCup is its initialisation as a new instance of the Container class. The identifier 'new' is an example of a selector which, when applied to an object/class, selects the required operations. The nature of a Container is that it can contain many different objects:

```
[pencilCup add: [Pen blue]]
```

The selector add: adds extra items to the collection, where the item to be added follows the selector. One adds, therefore, an instance of the Pen class to the collection in the container, and the selector blue directs that the instance is that of a blue Pen. It is possible to add: (without special programming) other instances from other classes of object, thus easing production of code.

New classes are defined by giving the new ClassName and (possibly) a SuperClassName which is the class from which the new class will inherit all instance variables, instance methods, and factory methods. Objective-C provides techniques for defining methods appropriate to a specified class, implemented as selectors (messages). For example, the method/selector pair x: y: used with, say, the class Point can be defined by

```
+ x: (int) anX y: (int) aY
  {
```

```
self = [self new];
xLoc = anX;
yLoc = aY;
return self;
}
```

The + is an indication that this method is to be used to define an instance of a class (a 'factory' method). The two selectors are x: and y: which take the int parameters anX and aY. These parameters are used in the method definition which follows. If the line were prefixed by a minus then the method would be an instance method, used for defining methods for existing instances.

self is a pseudo instance which points to the Point class, and [self new] creates a new uninitialised instance of Point and returns the new instance. The line self = [self new] takes the new instance of the class defined, and self is assigned to itself. This means that the method applies to the instance and not the class as a whole. Within the class definition a Point is given two internal states xLoc and yLoc, and the values of the arguments are assigned to these internal states. The injunction return self is an instruction to return the value of the instance.

The full impact of the combination of such techniques is perhaps easier to appreciate in combination with other object-using programming environments such as Digital Research's GEM (Graphics Environment Manager).

Interactive C programming

When discussing the production of C programs we have had to examine the multiple steps needed to move from source code to executable object code.

If you examine C you will notice that a program is composed of a large number of functions which might be separately compiled, and executed as part of program testing (removing the primacy of the main( ) function). A very good implementation of an interactive system is Instant-C (from Rational Systems, Inc), and this is the version I will use for my discussion.

The Instant-C system hinges on three environments

1. The interpreter
This is the part of the system which reads in the user's commands, executing the commands directly or via the Instant-C debugger. Some interpreter commands activate the editor, others will activate your program. As with most interpreters, the input is executed one line at a time. The interpreter environment is signalled by a # prompt.

2. The editor
As the name suggests this is an editor (but a full-screen editor, not a line editor), which is used for manipulating C language source text. The editor acts on input one character at a time. The editor is entered either by use of

the #ed NAME command in the interpreter, or as a result of the compiler finding a syntax error in a C source language file. There is no prompt in editor mode.

3. Program execution

A program is executed by typing a valid function called whilst in the interpreter. To run a complete program, for example, the user enters

```
# main();
```

which will produce the same effect as is normally achieved when executing a C executable code program. To test an individual function, for example, one enters

```
# activate(negOp);
```

and program execution will terminate when any of the following is true:

1. The program makes a call to exit or _exit.
2. The function invoked in the interpreter encounters a return, or reaches the end of the function.
3. A breakpoint set within the program is encountered.
4. A function for which the trace facility has been activated is called or returns.
5. The program completes a statement whilst the user is single stepping through the program.
6. The program makes a runtime error.
7. The program is interrupted by use of CTRL C.

One very useful aspect of an interactive system such as Instant-C is that programs can readily be developed and debugged, and then once the program is working the source code files can be recompiled by an optimising compiler to speed execution. Instant-C programs require the C compiler to be present in memory for the program to execute, but there is a facility to produce stand alone programs.

Though not really comparable, there are BASIC systems (for example) which allow the interactive development of BASIC programs which can then be compiled – once the interpreted version is working correctly. The only problem is compatibility between interpreters and compilers, because often interpreters provide facilities which are difficult to implement in a compiler. As Instant-C has moved from a compiler system to an interpreter, the compatibility problems are lessened in that respect. Problems of compatibility are only likely to arise from differences between compilers.

Making C live

Living C is another interactive version of C, but with a big difference. The difference is that C lives by enabling the user to step through a C program: the stepping is not that of a trace function, but an element by element analysis of each line.

The stepping through the program can be controlled from very slow to fast to a line at a time, to no stepping at all. With Living C it is possible to

- Selectively monitor a variable to see how the variable's value changes as the program executes.
- Stop the program either by hitting the Break key or by setting break points in the program.

Variables can be examined, values can be changed, or the program can be edited and re-executed to evaluate the changes.

When a program is executed several windows are active. In one window the output from the program is shown, and in another is the program text with a cursor showing the program in progress (i.e. living). Watching the cursor as it steps through a program instruction can be very instructive, because the cursor follows the way in which each instruction is parsed by the C translator. In Varith the parsing was very elementary, being merely a conversion to reverse Polish notation, but in the Living C translator (as with all translators for large systems) the parsing is based on a tree structure (see the appendix on BCPL, as the parse tree is one of the explicit stages of BCPL code generation).

For example, to use an instruction given in the Living C Personal manual (from Living Software Ltd):

    a = b + c

is converted into a tree

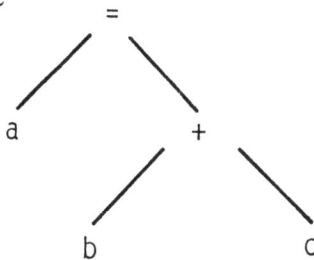

which can also be written as the line

    = a + b c

and this is the order in which the instruction is executed. The cursor follows this pattern:

1. Go to 'assign operator' (cursor on =).
2. Calculate the address of the left-hand side (cursor goes to a).
3. Calculate the right-hand side (cursor on +).

4. Get value of left-hand operand of + (cursor on b).
5. Get value of right-hand operand (cursor on c).

To assist in the development of programs, taking particular note of the problem of errors in programs, when Living C compiles a program it will

- Flag errors, one at a time, as they are detected.
- Show on screen the position of the error in the original source code program.
- Provide on-screen help on the nature of the error and possible causes.

It is possible to use the Living C editor to correct the error, and then continue compilation.

Living C depends on a resident compiler for its action. Once Living C programs execute correctly then those programs can be compiled using other systems (as with Instant-C). As the Living C environment is such a powerful means of investigating and learning C, the Varith source has been modified to run under Living C and can be obtained from Living Software Ltd with the Living C package for no extra cost. When ordering Living C, therefore, ask for the Varith source files.

Appendix A
BCPL - An Outline

BCPL was designed by Martin Richards in 1967. It was changed fairly substantially in its early stages, but has remained reasonably stable for many years.

BCPL has a strong following from many of those influenced by work at various British universities, but it is of note that in 1969 Dennis Ritchie of Bell Laboratories wrote (with R. H. Canaday) a BCPL programming manual[1]. The same Dennis Ritchie is the coauthor (with Brian Kernighan) of the bible of C[2] which was published at about the same time as the bible of BCPL[3]. The two languages are thus intimately connected: in the BCPL text, reference is made explicitly to work in C; furthermore, in an internal Bell Laboratories report by Ritchie et al[4], the authors remark that:

> The C language in use today is the product of several years of evolution. Many of its most important ideas stem from the considerably older, but still quite vital, language BCPL developed by Martin Richards. The influence of BCPL on C proceeded indirectly through the language B, which was written by Ken Thompson in 1970 for the first UNIX system on the PDP-11.

Building BCPL

Richards' original reason for developing BCPL was the creation of a compiler writing tool. The language took some ideas from CPL (Combined Programming Language), a programming language developed at the universities of Cambridge and London. CPL had tried to be a language which offered a very rich selection of control mechanisms, and thus presented an elegant means of programming. The aim of BCPL was to try to keep most of this richness whilst at the same time aiming for an efficiency of use that was necessary for systems programming. This meant that BCPL had to be less complex and less general than CPL or many other languages.

This description shows that the design aims of BCPL correspond closely to the avowed aims of C, though one aim of C is to be somewhat more general than BCPL. The truth of the matter is that ultimately BCPL is every bit as general as C, but C is simpler to write because C has extra facilities which add to its ease of use. By the same token, C is also more difficult to write than BCPL because of these extra facilities. Here is one of the classic confusions in programming in that most languages can be persuaded to do most things, given time and effort, but certain languages are better equipped than others to ease programming of specific types of application. Even so, we find that Richard Bornat, in his book on compiler writing[5], makes slight alterations to BCPL to assist in his task of explaining how compilers are written, thus even the compiler writer can be modified for writing about compiler writing. Bornat says of BCPL:

> I've used BCPL as the language of illustration throughout most of this book because it is designed as a special system programming language and is especially suited to the special problems of compiler writing ... [but] I have taken many liberties with BCPL syntax in examples, mainly inspired by the need to compress complicated algorithms into the space of a single page.

One key aspect of BCPL (and one which has carried over to Small-C-80 in particular) is that the compiler for BCPL was written in BCPL. BCPL was, therefore, ahead of its time in this respect as well as in others, because the notion (though not novel) had not previously been given such a considered examination. It is interesting to note that, for example, Pascal used a similar idea to ease implementation of the Pascal compiler: the Pascal compiler was also written in Pascal, and Pascal P-code became a popular implementation tool on microcomputers[6]. The BCPL compiler works in three stages.

1. The source code program, written in standard BCPL, is analysed for its grammatical (or syntactical) correctness. The result of this analysis (if the program is grammatically correct) is an intermediate form of BCPL known as the 'applicative tree', which is the program stored in a form that is easier for the next stage of the compiler to analyse. The applicative tree turns the standard BCPL source into a structure which can be used for computation: at an elementary level, for example, the arithmetic statement '2 + 3' is turned into the reverse Polish form ' 2 3 +' (and so forth). The construction of the applicative tree is known as the 'syntactic phase'.
2. In the next stage of compilation the applicative tree is translated into another intermediate form of BCPL called OCODE. OCODE can be regarded as the assembly language for an idealised BCPL machine (see below for a description of this machine). An example of an OCODE translation (taken from Richards and Whitby-Strevens) is is the BCPL assignment:

X := V!2

which is translated into the OCODE commands:

LN 2	load the constant 2
LG 100	and load V
PLUS	add these two values together
RV	indirect one level (that is, find the value stored in location V+2)
SP 3	store the result in X

where the value of V is stored in cell 100, V!2 is the content of the cell whose address is V+2, and the value of X is stored in cell 3. The assignment means: store the value of the content of cell V+2 in the variable X. The production of the OCODE program is known as the 'translation phase', and note that in this example the addition 'V + 2' will have been translated in the syntactic phase to '2 V +'.

3. The final stage of the compilation is the generation of 'target code' for the real (physical) machine by conversion of OCODE into the real computer's machine code. To implement BCPL on a new computer, therefore, only the OCODE language need be turned into machine code. This phase is called 'code generation', and to transfer BCPL to a new machine it is necessary to write a new code generator. To assist in the transfer of BCPL to new machines a new assembly language, better suited than OCODE, has been specifically developed – it is known as INTCODE.

The BCPL compilation system depends upon the idealised BCPL machine, so this is our next concern.

The BCPL machine

The idealised computer on which BCPL operates was chosen to make the language both portable and easy to define accurately. An idealised machine has no real existence, for it is no more than a convenient abstraction designed to ease the construction of the language and its compiler. The language compiler is designed to correspond to this particular machine, so that, when faced with a real machine, the implementer has only to convert from the assembly language of the ideal machine to the assembly language of the real machine. The conversion from one assembly language to another is less work than the production of a complete compiler, especially if the ideal assembly language is chosen to assist in the conversion.

The BCPL idealised machine has a 'store', which is no more than a set of numbered storage cells arranged so that the numbers labelling consecutive cells differ by the value 1. Each storage cell holds a bit pattern (that is, a binary number whose bits are individually specifiable), where the bit pattern is known as a value. All storage cells are the same size (unlike C), and their size depends on the computer on which the language is implemented – a cell is the equivalent of a computer 'word'. The only object that BCPL can manipulate directly is the value stored in a cell: all variables and expressions have to relate to one of these values.

Though there is only one overt type of value in BCPL, what such a value represents depends upon the programmer (as often happens with C). There is only one internal type, the bit pattern, but there are many possible conceptual types (that is, types designated by the programmer): a value may be an integer, or a character, or part of a multilength number, or any such item. The most important implications of having only one internal type in the design of a language (and the same is true of FORTH) are given by Richards and Whitby-Strevens as the following:

1. There is no need for type declarations (as with the Algols or Pascal) because the internal type of every variable is already known. This clarity of type tends to make programs more concise, and removes many problems which arise with the mismatching of types in assignments or in the passing of parameters to procedures.
2. The power of BCPL with only one internal data type is almost as great as a language (such as Pascal) with dynamically changing types. As the type is always known, the computational efficiency of BCPL is as great as a language (such as FORTRAN) which has specific, fixed, data types. This is due to the fact that though the internal type of a variable is always known, its conceptual type is infinitely variable. Languages where the elements of arrays must have the same type, for example, have to implement novel devices to handle dynamically varying data structures (e.g. variant records in Pascal).
3. As BCPL possesses only one internal type there is no need for the compiler to perform automatic type checking, thus it is always possible for the user to write silly programs which will still be compiled successfully. As with FORTH, speed and flexibility is bought at the expense of security for the unwary.

One of the important ideas BCPL takes from CPL is the distinction between a variable and a manifest constant (this distinction is copied by C, though using different terms). A *variable*, on the one hand, is a name which is associated with a storage cell, and a variable has a value, the contents of that cell. The value of a variable may be altered in the course of a program by an assignment command. A *manifest constant*, on the other hand, is the direct association of a name with a value. The association of the value with the name occurs at compile time, and is constant throughout the execution of a program.

There are two subtypes of variable:

Static variables A 'global' variable whose extent is the entire execution of the program. The storage cell is allocated prior to execution and continues to exist until execution is complete.

Dynamic variables A 'local' variable whose extent commences with the appropriate declaration and ends when the scope of that declaration is exited.

The START of BCPL

The key procedure in a BCPL program is START because, when a BCPL program is executed, the program begins by calling the procedure START (compare the use of <u>main</u> in C). A procedure definition in BCPL is just one form of a declaration, and all declarations in BCPL start with the keyword LET, then the name and an assignment operator, followed by the value to which the name is initialised. Assignment operators vary, and in the case of a procedure the assignment operator is BE. The initial value of a procedure is its definition, and the initial value of a variable is the content of the cell to which the variable refers.

Here is a declaration of a procedure START (taken, with no claims for originality, from Richards and Whitby-Strevens):

```
LET START() BE WRITES("Hello readers")
```

A declaration starts with LET, the name declared is START, and the value is initialised to BE the instruction WRITES ("Hello readers"). WRITES () is a procedure (WRITE String) which will output the value of the string given as parameter: note that to print the value of a variable considered as a number the procedure is different, that is, WRITEN() (WRITE Number). BCPL, as with C, has specific procedures to perform specific tasks.

The procedures WRITES() and WRITEN() are assumed to be contained in a special program library known, say, as LIBHDR, and to load the library for use we GET "LIBHDR". Here is a simple program:

```
GET "LIBHDR"
LET START() BE
    $( LET A, B = 1, 2
       A := A + B
       WRITES("Sum of A and B is ")
       WRITEN(A)
    $)
```

which can be rewritten using manifest constants as:

```
GET "LIBHDR"
MANIFEST $( ONE = 1; TWO = 2 $)
LET START() BE
    $( LET A, B = ONE, TWO
```

```
        A := A + B
        WRITES("Sum of A and B is ")
        WRITEN(A)
    $)
```

or, slightly altered:

```
GET "LIBHDR"
MANIFEST $( ONE = 1; TWO = 2 $)
LET START() BE
    $( LET A, B = ONE, TWO
       A := A + B
       WRITEOUT(A)
    $)

AND WRITEOUT(X) BE
    $( WRITES("Sum of two numbers is ")
       WRITEN(X)
    $)
```

This is a segment of program in which there are two declarations START() and WRITEOUT(X). This outline only scratches the surface of the use of procedures in BCPL, but is sufficient, I hope, to give some idea of the nature of the language and declarations. Note that instead of the more prolix BEGIN and END of some languages, BCPL has the section brackets '$(' and '$)' which can be nested as with BEGIN and END. At any point where a simple command in BCPL is allowed there can be a complex command, that is, more than one simple command enclosed in $(and $).

Commands are separated in BCPL either by being on a new line, or by having an intervening semicolon (if more than one command is on the same line). A command can spread over more than one line if the break in the command is at some point at which it is impossible to complete a command. For example, the first assignment below is correct, whereas the second assignment will produce a syntax error:

```
A := B +
    C

A := B
    + C
```

because A := B is a legal command, whereas the command A := B + is incomplete.

Condition and control

Before moving to examine the way in which memory and values are arranged in BCPL, here is a list of the manifold means by which computation can be controlled in BCPL. In the following, 'expr' is some BCPL expression which then is evaluated for its truth (true is a nonzero value), and 'comm' is some BCPL command.

IF expr THEN comm
If the expression is true then execute that command.

UNLESS expr DO comm
If the expression is false then execute that command.

TEST expr THEN comm1 ELSE comm2
If the expression is true then execute the first command, else execute the second command.

WHILE expr DO comm
While the expression is true, execute the command continually.

UNTIL expr DO comm
Until the expression is true, execute the command continually.

comm REPEAT
Execute the command continually, without end.

comm REPEATWHILE expr
Execute the command at least once, and then continually, while the expression is true.

comm REPEATUNTIL expr
Execute the command at least once, and then continually, until the expression is true.

FOR n = expr1 TO expr2 BY k DO comm
For values of n from expr1 to expr2 in steps of k, execute the command.

FOR n = expr1 TO expr2 DO comm
For values of n from expr1 to expr2 in steps of 1, execute the command.

VALOF $(comm1 RESULTIS expr comm2 $)
The compound within the $(to $) limits is executed until a RESULTIS command is encountered (usually as part of some conditional command). For example, IF C > 100 RESULTIS C might be used in the definition of a function to find the value of the first number greater than 100 (where a function returns a result and a procedure just performs some action). A simple example is:

```
LET MAX(N1, N2) = VALOF
   $( TEST N1 > N2 THEN RESULTIS N1
                   ELSE RESULTIS N2 )$
```

or more complex:

```
LET OVER100() = VALOF
  $( LET C = 0
     $( C := READN() ; IF C > 100 RESULTIS C $)
        REPEAT
  $)
```

which finds the first number in a sequence which is greater than 100 (the numbers are read from some device). Note that BCPL introduced the idea that input and output were functions and procedures on a par with other functions and procedures.

SWITCHON expr INTO $(CASE A : commA ENDCASE; ... ; DEFAULT : comm ENDCASE $)
This is a command which simplifies multiway testing, and is common in other languages.

It can be seen that the means for controlling program execution in BCPL are extensive almost to excess. Ritchie et al [1978/1980] make the valid point that:

> It is interesting that BCPL provided these instructions in 1967, well before the current vogue for 'structured programming'.

The possession of such a wide and powerful set of contructs is reflected in the design of C, though – obviously – the exact forms of these control structures will differ between the languages.

Vectors and indirection

The idealised machine with BCPL gives great power, because each variable name is associated with an address. For any variable NAME there is an ADDRESS, where ADDRESS := @NAME. A variable has a VALUE where VALUE is produced by giving the NAME, or by VALUE := !ADDRESS. If the value of NAME is equal to ADDRESS2, then !NAME will give the value stored at ADDRESS2.

It is easy to see how useful such flexibility can be in the manipulation of values, and the clearest example of this flexibility can be found in the treatment of arrays in BCPL. An array in BCPL can have only one dimension, and such arrays are termed vectors. To declare a 10 element vector, V, the command is:

```
LET V = VEC 9
```

That is, declare the vector (V) to have one less (9) than the desired number of elements (10), because the vector is indexed from element 0 to the maximum element specified (9). The elements of V are distinguished by V!0 V!1 V!2 ... V!9, and the meaning of the 'pling' (!) is the one we have already encountered in that it means the value stored at the specified address.

The meaning of V!INDEX is !(V + INDEX), that is, the value stored in the location V + INDEX. In BCPL, not only are the elements of a vector selected by consecutive numbers (that is, V!0 V!1 ...) but also the values are stored in consecutive memory cells. Thus the first element of the vector V is stored at address V, and the final element (V!9) is stored at address 9 + V. As V!INDEX is equivalent to !(V + INDEX) then V!0 is equivalent to !(V + 0), or to !V. The treatment of vectors is thus completely consistent, and the general technique by which the elements of the vector are isolated is known as 'indirection' (the ! is the indirection operator).

As it is possible to access addresses as values of cells, where the address is of a cell which can also contain an address ('pointers' to other cells), this gives a great deal of flexibility. This means, however, that if an address is 16 bits, then the size of a cell has to be 16 bits, unless special techniques are employed. One reason why C has a greater number of types comes from the restrictions which the BCPL idealised machine place on access to memory. On most minicomputers (and nearly all microcomputers) memory is byte addressable, that is, the primitive memory storage unit is 8 bits, with more than one byte to a computer cell (or word). With the idealised BCPL machine it is very difficult to use the byte facilities of the physical machine (to stop many program inefficiencies).

A further problem with the classic BCPL word oriented idealised machine is that with the memory of a real machine organised as bytes (say, two bytes to a cell) the expression V!1 will not produce the address of the next cell but rather the address of the next byte, unless the effect of the operation of ! is modified or an extra indirection operator (say, ?) is available to distinguish between word indirection and byte indirection. It is worth noting that in BBC BASIC there are many BCPL influenced facilities, and BBC BASIC offers two forms of indirection (indicated by ! and ?).

For this reason, and others concerning changing forms of memory organisation and the impact of hardware implementations of floating point arithmetic, C incorporated types. One beneficial result of the BCPL concentration on memory cells organised in a regular manner was the introduction into the BCPL language of special functions for the manipulation of bits within values (that is, bit patterns).

BCPL and C

Ritchie et al [1978/1980] give four ways in which the languages BCPL, B, and C, have common characteristics. We will concentrate on BCPL and C in the comparison.

1. All the languages are able to use a full complement of control constructs, in which is included the ability to provide meaningful ways to group statements (for example, the $(and$) pair in BCPL, and the ⟨ and ⟩ pair in C, allow local variables).
2. All three include the concept of a 'pointer' (an address stored as a value), and provide means by which addresses can be manipulated.
3. Arguments (parameters) to functions and procedures are passed by value and not by name, so that any modification of a parameter value within a procedure does not affect the parameter value outside the scope of the procedure. Call by name is possible by passing a pointer to a value, and explicity changing that value.
4. The languages are all rather low level in that they deal with the same types of object as do real computers. BCPL restricts its attention to machine words (cells) whilst C includes characters, multiword integers (possibly) and floating point numbers. None of the languages deals directly with composites such as character strings, sets, lists, or arrays considered as a unit. I/O is not part of any of these languages, and such facilities have to be provided by special routines called from libraries.

The final similarity I would like to emphasise is one which Ritchie et al omit, and an aspect of BCPL which I have not mentioned so far. The similarity concerns the separate compilation of program modules and the linking together of these modules, one of the keys to C's success. Richards and Whitby-Strevens note:

> When you first design a program, design in separate compilation from the beginning (which is also a good programming discipline) even if the modules are only half a page long. Put the global and manifest required throughout the program into a separate file and use GET at the head of each module.

Thus BCPL instigated the concern with the modular decomposistion of problems so important to C (which uses #include), and the separate compilation facilities of C have been a very important reason for the success of both BCPL and C.

No language can be perfect, so we will leave BCPL with its most famous ambiguity of meaning. The command to analyse is:

```
WHILE expr1 DO comm REPEATUNTIL expr2
```

This command can mean either:

```
WHILE expr1 DO $( comm REPEATUNTIL expr2 $)
```

or:

```
$( WHILE expr1 DO comm $) REPEATUNTIL expr2
```

Which interpretation do you prefer?

References

[1] R. H. Canaday and D. M. Ritchie, *The BCPL programming manual*, Bell Laboratories (1969).

[2] B. W. Kernighan and D. M. Ritchie, *The C programming language*, Prentice-Hall (1978).

[3] M. Richards and C. Whitby-Strevens, *BCPL, the language and its compiler*, Cambridge University Press (1979).

[4] D. M. Ritchie, S. C. Johnson, M. E. Lesk and B. W. Kernighan, *The C programming language*, Bell Laboratories (1978), reprinted in Dr Dobbs Journal (1980).

[5] R. Bornat, *Understanding and writing compilers*, Macmillan Press (1979).

[6] B. Allan, *Introducing Pascal*, Collins Professional and Technical Books (1984).

Appendix B
UNIX - An Outline

In any book concerning the UNIX operating system there needs to be a section about C, and in any book concerning C there needs to be a section about UNIX. C and UNIX are intertwined because C is the language of the UNIX operating system.

The use of the UNIX operating system does not always imply the use of the C programming language, because when using UNIX it is perfectly possible to get by without using C. For example, by using UNIX only for word processing one might never need to program in any language (though such a specific concentration is unlikely). In a similar manner, the use of the C programming language certainly does not imply the use of the UNIX operating system. For example, possibly the biggest growth in the use of C has been in the microcomputer arena, and usually microcomputers use conventional operating systems which have very little in common with UNIX.

Even with 'conventional' operating systems on microcomputers, however, the influence of UNIX is apparent. For example, the MSDOS operating system from Microsoft has many UNIX-like features; in fact Microsoft's XENIX operating system uses the original UNIX source (licenced from AT&T) with only slight modifications/improvements.

The above are the key aspects of the UNIX operating system, in what I consider to be the appropriate order of importance for the user rather than the UNIX expert. Jokingly, Carl Phillips says that the key aspect of UNIX is that 'It works', and that a subsidiary benefit is that UNIX helps reach the parts other operating systems cannot reach. There is a great deal of sense in his assertions, and these two aspects of UNIX are also key aspects of C. This equivalence is a result of the history of UNIX and C, in that both were developed by small teams of enthusiasts to help the developers in their own work: UNIX and C were developed by research scientists, and were not planned from on high.

UNIX was designed to be a flexible working system but, like C, it was not a system for the lowest common denominator in programmers. The flexibility and programmability of UNIX are best illustrated by four facilities:

- I/O redirection
- Piping
- Hierachical files
- The shell

As I do not intend to give a comprehensive outline of UNIX I will concentrate on these four aspects, and in the final section will consider some rather more general points about the use of UNIX. Before looking at UNIX, it is as well to consider what is the purpose of an operating system, and the difference between an operating system, an environment, and a programming language.

What is an operating system?

Or: what distinguishes an operating system from a programming language?

If one considers machine code as being the ultimate end point of computer operation, in that computers function by executing sequences of instructions expressed as machine code, then an operating system is the ultimate starting point of computer operation. Programming languages occupy various points along the continuum from machine code to operating system, and some operating systems overlap in their capabilities with some programming languages.

The difference between an operating system, a programming language, and machine code is best illustrated by how each copes with the peripherals and devices attached to the computer. For example, control of a device (say, a printer) by use of machine code programs is often accomplished by depositing information in specific computer locations according to specific rules. An ordinary programming language usually controls a device (say, the printer) by name, without the user having to know anything about how the device works. An operating system, however, will frequently allow the printer to reflect what is being output on the screen, so that the printer is only one of a range of possible interchangeable devices (including disk files).

The extensiveness of an operating system is reflected in the system's ability to control the devices available to the programmer. The more powerful and more extensive the operating system, the fewer the facilities for input and output needed by any programming language. UNIX has many facilities (indeed an abundance) for controlling the operation of the system, and this is reflected in the remarkably simple facilities for input and output present in C. C is a very low level programming language (as with BCPL), whereas UNIX is a very high level operating system.

I/O redirection

The UNIX program ls lists the names of files in the current directory (on some UNIX systems the ls program is called dir), so that the command

$ ls

will display details of the files in the directory, together with information about the status of each file. The $ is the system prompt, which can be varied at the user's behest, and is only shown here to distinguish information entered by the user from screen output (though screen output is only relevant for our purposes in the discussion of the shell). The display is to the screen, and to copy that information to a printer we 'redirect' the screen output to the disk file lsfile by

$ ls > lsfile

where the redirection operator $>$ indicates that the output from the command to the left is to be sent to the file named to right of the output operator, $>$. This facility is very general, and its limits depend upon the physical configuration of the computer installation, that is, the devices to which the computer is connected.

The command wc can be used (without parameters) to count the number of characters input from the standard input device. To count the number of characters in the file lsfile, it is possible to treat lsfile as equivalent to the standard input by use of the input redirection operator $<$. Thus enter

$ wc < lsfile

and the result goes to the standard output device. This can be redirected to a file lswcfile

$ wc < lsfile > lswcfile

or, alternatively

$ wc > lswcfile < lsfile

because the order is immaterial. There are three standard 'files' available with UNIX:

- Standard input
- Standard output
- Standard error output

which correspond exactly to the files STDIN, STDOUT, and STDERR used in C.

In C, therefore, to redirect output from the standard output to a file of a different name it is possible either to change the file designation within C or to redirect the standard output at the level of UNIX. Obviously we need to be able to change the output channel from within C, because sometimes we wish to send output to more than one output channel (that is, to a different file). However, the facility to redirect output (and input) at the level of the operating system is an extra, and very helpful, facility not available to all operating systems.

Piping

We have just developed a sequence

```
$ ls > lsfile
$ wc < lsfile > lswcfile
```

which lists file names, sending the output to file lsfile, and which then counts the number of lines, words, and characters in the file lsfile, sending the output to the file lswcfile. A similar sequence is

```
$ ls > lsfile
$ wc -w < lsfile > lswcfile
```

which counts only the number of words in the file lsfile (because each word corresponds to one file name). The parameter (or'option')–w indicates that only words are to be counted. On some UNIX systems, each file name is on a separate line so that the count of words is equal to the count of lines, but on other systems more than one file name appears on a line. The listing in this latter case contains as many lines as are needed to list all the names.

If the command line is

```
$ wc -wl < lsfile
```

or, alternatively

```
$ wc -w -l < lsfile
```

then by comparing the two numbers (output to the standard device) one can tell, without looking at the listing, whether there is one name per line (in which case the numbers have the same value).

The UNIX program who provides information concerning how many people are using the system, one user to a line. To find this number of people we enter

```
$ who > whofile
$ wc -l < whofile > whowcfile
$ cat whowcfile
```

where the new command cat lists a file to the standard output file (usually the screen, or possibly a teletype). If a series of file names is provided then the files are concatenated, that is, one file is listed directly after another: if the standard output is redirected to a file then the files are physically concatenated.

We need the intermediate files (especially, in the last case, whofile) for the intermediate storage of information, but this is intrinsically rather wasteful. Once we have the whofile and have used it with wc, we are unlikely to need whofile again. The file whowcfile is not necessary because we can lose a line by not redirecting, thus

```
$ who > whofile
$ wc -l < whofile
```

will list the number of lines in the whofile onto the standard output device.
There is a shorter method:

```
$ who | wc -1
```

which uses the technique known as 'piping' – like a pipe the contents move
from one end to another. The initial content of the pipe is the list of users
produced by who; this content then passes down the pipe to be accepted as
the input to the next command. The output of wc −1 is the final content and
passes to the standard output device (unless redirected). Piping can be
extended well beyond two stages, for example

```
$ who | sort | lpr
```

will find who is attached to the system, sort their names into alphabetical
order, take the sorted output, and send the results to be printed as a
'background' job (that is, the printing will not interfere with your other
UNIX work).

By appending & to a pipe sequence the complete job can be turned into
one which will run in the background. For example, if there are a great
number of users, sorting into alphabetical order may take a good deal of
time, so the sorting is best performed whilst you are getting on with other
things:

```
$ who | sort | lpr -m &
```

As can be appreciated, piping is just one form of programming, and (given
the great number of UNIX facilities) a powerful form of programming – the
−m option to lpr is used to send 'mail' to you when the printing is complete.
The electronic mail facilities of UNIX have all kinds of uses and utilities and
are employed a great deal.

Hierachical directories

At every point of development of C and UNIX (remembering that UNIX is
written in C) the desire was to produce a conceptual simplification in the
operation of the system. The functioning of UNIX (and any other operating
system of worth) depends heavily on the use of files of information. With a
large system, therefore, there are likely to be many users, each with many
files.

If there are a large number of files, therefore, it is quite possible that there
will be many duplicate file names: for example, 'test' is such a common
notion that there will be many users who will wish to use the name test for a
test file. If the files are stored in one unorganised mass, every time a user sets
up a file known as test, this will erase the contents of any earlier file of that
name – a file which may be needed later by its originator. The obvious way
to prevent such mayhem is to give each user a specific disk memory

allocation, on which the user can save files unaffected by other users (each user may then have a file known as test, where only the user who has created that version of the file can modify it).

There are further problems, however, due to the need for users to share information and perhaps use each other's files. There has to be a mechanism which allows such sharing of files, and so operating systems developed facilities to allow access to the files of other users. This access had to be controlled by the originator of the file, thus the systems developed complicated mechanisms to control the extent to which users could use other files, and under what conditions. Files were effectively classed as R/W (read and write), R/O (read only), or P (private or protected).

However, when programmers began to work in groups on a project all of them had information to share, but at the same time the group members did not want people from outside the group to share the (possibly confidential) information. All the users in that group could therefore be given the same user identification, but the same problems arose with contamination of information, with large numbers of programmers all wanting to call their files test. One response to this problem is the institution of what on some systems is called PPNs (Project, Programmer Numbers) thus the group has a project number, and each programmer within the group has a distinct identification.

Within each project grouping, we have the same situation as before with users who can decide on the status of access to their files. Of course, on large projects a user might have a file called test for one aspect of his work but, when dealing with another aspect, use the name test without realising that the name already exists. Really it would seem that a system ought to provide a user with distinct areas of memory for each aspect of his application (with the user controlling his own rights of access to each subset of files).

If you examine the progression from anarchy through project area to user aspect area, at each stage we have a portion of memory which is divided into discrete segments, all of equal status. We have produced a hierachy of file storage, but the system is slightly ad hoc and inconsistent. UNIX treats each area as a disk file, with subsidiary disk files within each disk file. At the highest level there is the UNIX filestore (the 'root' directory) divided into subfiles, one of which is normally known as 'usr'. The usr subdirectory will itself contain subdirectories, some of which contain private user files, where the content of each individual subdirectory is itself a file. Each private user file (which may be shared by a group of users, as with a project designation) can itself have private user files, or subdirectories. When you log in to UNIX you are in your 'home' directory (a subdirectory of usr), and your home directory contains the files you feel you need most frequently.

For each particular personal project in which you are engaged you can create subdirectories. When the contents of the directory are listed you will find ordinary files and special directory files. Each of the special directory files will contain information about the files in that subdirectory, whether those files be normal files or subdirectories themselves. To get to any file within any subdirectory you specify a pathname. For example, to get to a file 'readme', which is in a subdirectory 'info' of the subdirectory 'help' of the home directory 'ba001', we change the directory by cd:

```
$ cd /usr/ba001/help/infoC
cat readme
```

and we are in the infoC subdirectory, and listing readme. Suppose we would like to have information about BCPL, information which is contained in the subdirectory 'infoBCPL ' of the subdirectory 'help'. If we move back one level from infoC we are back to help, so we issue the command

```
$ cat ../infoBCPL/readme
```

where the two dots .. mean go up a level from the subdirectory (we are still in the infoC subdirectory because we have not issued a cd command). To get back to the ba001 subdirectory from infoC, the command is

```
$ cd ../../
```

that is, go back two levels in the hierarchy.

Each file (or subdirectory) can have its own 'permissions', which are codes that establish the access rights of others to your files. The permissions are reproduced by use of the −l option to ls, and the permissions are in three classes: the 'user', the members of the 'group' (where membership of the group is given from above by the system 'superuser'), and 'others'. There are three forms of permission for each of the three classes: the directory contents may be listed, the directory entries may be created or removed, and directory entries may be accessed or the directory may be the subject of a cd command. With each set of permissions there is also an indication of whether the entry is that of a subdirectory or an ordinary file.

The shell

Though you have seen a few standard UNIX commands, these commands are not (in a sense) 'UNIX' commands. The commands are those from the standard UNIX shell. The shell is so called because it is a protective layer around the soft centre which is UNIX.

We communicate with UNIX via the shell, and it is possible to construct other shells to change the form of communication with UNIX. A very popular shell is that from the University of California at Berkeley, known variously as the C shell or the Berkeley shell, where the shell commands are closely related to the syntax of the C language.

It is possible for the ordinary user to rewrite portions of his own shell by producing programs in the shell command language, which can then be executed as if they were standard shell commands. At a very simple level, it is possible to define a variable so that whenever the variable is given, there is an exact replacement of the variable with the defined content. For example

```
$ helpdir=/usr/ba001/help
```

defines the variable $helpdir as being equal to the text "/usr/ba001/help", so to list the file in that subdirectory we ask

```
$ ls $helpdir
```

but to ask for the infoBCPL subdirectory we ask

```
$ ls ${helpdir}/infoBCPL
```

The curly braces are used to distinguish the variable from other text. Another feature of the UNIX shell is the ability to construct programs which emulate and extend standard facilities. For example, we can produce a short shell program to arrange the users in alphabetical order (see above for details of the operation of the pipe)

```
echo 'who | sort | lpr -m &' > alphawho
```

The primes serve to distinguish the program text from a pipe command. If we enter

```
$ cat alphawho
who | sort | lpr -m &
$
```

it can be seen that the content of the file is the text string "who ¦ sort ¦ lpr −m &". To activate the shell program we enter

```
$ sh alphawho
```

where the 'sh' indicates we are using the standard UNIX (or Bourne) shell – Steve Bourne developed the standard UNIX shell for Bell Laboratories. Different shells use different shell program commands: for example, if we were using the C (or Berkeley) shell we would enter

```
$ csh alphawho
```

In other operating system environments these types of program are called 'batch' programs, and shell programs have their own special programming language constructs with loop constructs, conditionals, and multiway switches.

The range of commands available in UNIX is extensive, and a list of commands available in standard UNIX occupies several pages. Some of the most important for the C programmer are:

cb   The C program beautifier, which is a 'pretty print' utility.

cc   The C compiler, with options which allow different levels of compilation.

ed The UNIX editor which can be used for many purposes other than entering C program source code.

ld A loader, used to link compiled files.

lint A C program checker which is used to apply first aid to a C program. That is, lint applies support to a program by indicating to what extent some of the liberties taken with pointers and memory (say) are suspect.

pr A utility to print files.

UNIX clones and close clones

The Microsoft MSDOS system for microcomputers has facilities for the four key aspects of UNIX:

I/O redirection
MSDOS has facilities for I/O redirection which closely match those of UNIX.

Piping
The piping facilities in MSDOS are not as secure as those in UNIX because piping requires intermediate results to be are stored on disk, whereas with UNIX the virtual memory system assumes intermediate in memory. Some of the piping (and indirection) features are slightly insecure and not completely integrated in the non-UNIX aspects of MSDOS.

Hierachical files
There is provision for a system of hierarchical files which tries to emulate the UNIX system. The Microsoft C compiler makes extensive use of hierarchical files to organise the different types of files needed for a working C system.

The shell
The shell appears in two guises in MSDOS: the first (and conventional) guise is the provision of batch files with some C-like features; the second (and more interesting) is the CONFIG.SYS file which has facilities to allow the environment to be altered, and a special feature SHELL which enables the user to reprogram the user interface if desired.

There are many UNIX-like systems (going under a variety of names but usually ending with -IX), and at least one system (XENIX, from Microsoft) which is licenced from AT&T and is actually UNIX source. Renamed XENIX as part of the licence agreement, it appears on a variety of microcomputers; for example, Microsoft C can run under MSDOS or XENIX.

Appendix C
C Syntax

The definition of C syntax in the following pages is not intended as a strict or exact statement of the language; it is intended to assist users in understanding the language.

Any word in UPPER_CASE is not a part of the C language as such, and is ultimately defined in terms of basic items of the C language. All symbols are items within C, except the symbol $ which is used to indicate that the previous item or word is optional. The description of syntax is based on that given in Kernighan and Ritchie.

PREPROCESSOR_COMMANDS

```
#define IDENTIFIER TOKEN_STRING
#define IDENTIFIER ( IDENTIFIER, ...,
   IDENTIFIER ) TOKEN_STRING
#undef IDENTIFIER
#include "FILENAME"
#include <FILENAME>
#ifdef IDENTIFIER
#ifndef IDENTIFIER
#else
#endif
#line CONSTANT IDENTIFIER
```

PROGRAM

```
EXTERNAL_DEFINITION PROGRAM$
```

EXTERNAL_DEFINITION

```
FUNCTION_DEFINITION
DATA_DEFINITION
```

FUNCTION_DEFINITION

```
TYPE_SPECIFIER$ FUNCTION_DECLARATOR
   FUNCTION_BODY
```

FUNCTION_DECLARATOR

```
DECLARATOR ( PARAMETER_LIST$ )
```

PARAMETER_LIST

```
IDENTIFIER
IDENTIFIER , PARAMETER_LIST
```

```
FUNCTION_BODY

   TYPE_DECL_LIST FUNCTION_STATEMENT


FUNCTION_STATEMENT

   { DECLARATION_LIST$ STATEMENT_LIST }


DATA_DEFINITION

   extern$ TYPE_SPECIFIER$
      INIT_DECLARATOR_LIST$ ;
   static$ TYPE_SPECIFIER$
      INIT_DECLARATOR_LIST$ ;


COMPOUND_STATEMENT

   { DECLARATION_LIST$ STATEMENT_LIST$ }


DECLARATION_LIST

   DECLARATION DECLARATION_LIST$


STATEMENT_LIST

   STATEMENT STATEMENT_LIST$
```

STATEMENT

```
COMPOUND_STATEMENT
EXPRESSION ;
if ( EXPRESSION ) STATEMENT
if ( EXPRESSION ) STATEMENT else STATEMENT
while ( EXPRESSION ) STATEMENT
do STATEMENT while ( EXPRESSION ) ;
for ( EXPRESSION_1$ ; EXPRESSION_2$ ;
   EXPRESSION_3$) STATEMENT
switch (EXPRESSION ) STATEMENT
case CONSTANT_EXPRESSION : STATEMENT
default : STATEMENT
break ;
continue ;
return EXPRESSION$ ;
goto IDENTIFIER ;
IDENTIFIER : STATEMENT
;
```

DECLARATION

```
DECL_SPECIFIERS INIT_DECLARATOR_LIST$ ;
```

DECL_SPECIFIERS

```
TYPE_SPECIFIER DECL_SPECIFIERS$
SC_SPECIFIER DECL_SPECIFIERS$
```

SC_SPECIFIER

```
auto
static
extern
register
typedef
```

```
TYPE_SPECIFIER

    char
    short
    int
    long
    unsigned
    float
    double
    STRUCT_OR_UNION_SPECIFIER
    TYPEDEF_NAME


INIT_DECLARATOR_LIST

    INIT_DECLARATOR
    INIT_DECLARATOR , INIT_DECLARATOR_LIST


INIT_DECLARATOR

    DECLARATOR INITIALIZER$


DECLARATOR

    IDENTIFIER
    ( DECLARATOR )
    * DECLARATOR
    DECLARATOR ()
    DECALARATOR [ CONSTANT_EXPRESSION ]


STRUCT_OR_UNION_SPECIFIER

    struct { STRUCT_DECL_LIST }
    struct INDENTIFIER { STRUCT_DECL_LIST }
    struct INDENTIFIER
    union { STRUCT_DECL_LIST }
    union INDENTIFIER { STRUCT_DECL_LIST }
    union INDENTIFIER
```

STRUCT_DECL_LIST

    STRUCT_DECLARATION
    STRUCT_DECLARATION STRUCT_DECL_LIST$

STRUCT_DECLARATION

    TYPE_SPECIFIER STRUCT_DECLARATOR_LIST ;

STRUCT_DECLARATOR_LIST

    STRUCT_DECLARATOR
    STRUCT_DECLARATOR , STRUCT_DECLARATOR LIST

STRUCT_DECLARATOR

    DECLARATOR
    DECLARATOR$: CONSTANT_EXPRESSION

INITIALIZER

    = EXPRESSION
    = { INITIALIZER_LIST }
    = { INITIALIZER_LIST , }

INITIALIZER_LIST

    EXPRESSION
    INITIALIZER_LIST , INITIALIZER_LIST
    { INITIALIZER_LIST }

TYPE_NAME

    TYPE_SPECIFIER ABSTRACT_DECLARATOR

```
ABSTRACT_DECLARATOR

    EMPTY
    ( ABSTRACT_DECLARATOR )
    * ABSTRACT_DECLARATOR
    ABSTRACT_DECLARATOR ()
    ABSTRACT_DECLARATOR [ CONSTANT_EXPRESSION$ ]


TYPEDEF_NAME

    IDENTIFIER


EXPRESSION

    PRIMARY
    UNOP EXPRESSION
    INCOP LVALUE
    LVALUE INCOP
    EXPRESSION BINOP EXPRESSION
    EXPRESSION ? EXPRESSION : EXPRESSION
    LVALUE ASGNOP EXPRESSION
    EXPRESSION , EXPRESSION


PRIMARY

    IDENTIFIER
    CONSTANT
    STRING
    ( EXPRESSION )
    PRIMARY ( EXPRESSION_LIST$ )
    PRIMARY [ EXPRESSION ]
    LVALUE . IDENTIFIER
    PRIMARY -> IDENTIFIER
```

LVALUE

```
IDENTIFIER
PRIMARY [ EXPRESSION ]
LVALUE . IDENTIFIER
PRIMARY -> IDENTIFIER
* EXPRESSION
( LVALUE )
```

PRIMOP

```
( )
[ ]
.
->
```

All have highest (and equal) priority,
grouping left to right.

UNOP

```
*
&
-
!
~
INCOP
sizeof
( TYPE_NAME )
```

Have priority lower than that of the PRIMOPs,
but higher than any BINOP, they group right
to left.

INCOP

```
++
--
```

```
BINOP

   MULT_OP          Highest priority
   ADD_OP
   SHIFT_OP
   COMPARISON_OP
   EQUALITY_OP
   &
   ^
   |
   &&
   ||               Lowest priority.

   ?: has lower priority. Group left to right.


MULT_OP

   *
   /
   %


ADD_OP

   +
   -


SHIFT_OP

   >>
   <<


COMPARISON_OP

   <
   >
   <=
   >=
```

EQUALITY_OP

    ==
    !=

ASGNOP

    =
    +=
    -=
    *=
    /=
    %=
    >>=
    <<=
    &=
    ^=
    |=

    All have equal (and lowest) priority.

IDENTIFIER

    Sequence of characters beginning with a letter or underline.

CONSTANT_EXPRESSION

    INTEGER_CONSTANT
    FLOATING_POINT_CONSTANT
    CHARACTER_CONSTANT
    STRING_CONSTANT

INTEGER_CONSTANT

    DECIMAL_CONSTANT
    OCTAL_CONSTANT
    HEXADECIMAL_CONSTANT

DECIMAL_CONSTANT

Number not commencing with 0, optionally ending with l
or L to indicate a long value.

OCTAL_CONSTANT

Number (with digits from 0 to 7) commencing with 0,
optionally ending with l or L to indicate a long
value.

HEXADECIMAL_CONSTANT

Number (with digits 0 to 9, and characters a to f, or
A to F) commencing with 0x or 0X, optionally ending
with l or L to indicate a long value.

FLOATING_POINT_CONSTANT

DIGIT_SEQUENCE EXPONENT
DOTTED_DIGITS EXPONENT$

EXPONENT

A digit sequence commencing with e or E, and then an
optional + or -.

DOTTED_DIGITS

DIGIT_SEQUENCE .
DIGIT_SEQUENCE . DIGIT_SEQUENCE
. DIGIT_SEQUENCE

DIGIT_SEQUENCE

At least one digit.

CHARACTER_CONSTANT

       ' CHARACTER '

STRING_CONSTANT

    A (possibly empty) sequence of characters enclosed in
    " ".

CHARACTER

    PRINTING_CHARACTER
    ESCAPE_CHARACTER

ESCAPE_CHARACTER

    \ ESCAPE_CODE

ESCAPE_CODE

    CHARACTER_ESCAPE_CODE
    NUMERIC_ESCAPE_CODE

CHARACTER_ESCAPE CODE

    n
    t
    b
    r
    f
    v
    \
    '
    "

NUMERIC_ESCAPE_CODE

    A sequence of at least one and no more than three
    octal digits.

Appendix D
The Varith Source

The following pages contain listings of the Varith translator in the form in which they were compiled by Microsoft C. The source (and a compiled version of Varith running under MSDOS) can be obtained by writing to me via my publisher. The source can also be obtained on request (and free of charge) with the the Living C Personal system from Living Software Ltd.

```
/* Varith program */

/* Boris Allan */


#include "enVarith.h"

#include "lexToken.h"

#include "objTypes.h"

#include "rpnConv.h"

#include "exec.h"

main()

    {
    char inline[MAXBUFF], *store[MAXBUFF];
    int numToken, counter;

    initialize();

    while (lineIn(inline),
          strlen(inline) != 0)
        {

        numToken = makeTokens(inline,store);

        makeObjects(store,numToken);

        numToken = rpnMake(numToken);

        numToken = execRpn(numToken);

        printf("=> ");
        for (counter = 0;
             counter <= numToken ;
             counter++)
           printf("%d ",
                 valStack[counter].value);
        printf("\n");

        };
    }
```

```
/* enVarith.h file */

/* Boris Allan */


#include <string.h>

#include <stdio.h>

#include <ctype.h>

#define MAXBUFF 81

#define IDSIZE 10
```

```
/* lexToken.h file */

/* Boris Allan */


lineIn(buffer)

    char buffer[];

    {
        int counter, chval;

        for (counter = 0;
                counter < (MAXBUFF - 1) &&
                ((chval = getchar()) != EOF) &&
                (chval != '\n');
                counter++)
            buffer[counter] = chval;

        buffer[counter] = '\0';
        fflush(stdin);

    }

makeTokens(buffer,pc)

    char buffer[MAXBUFF], *pc[];

    {
        static char p[2*MAXBUFF];
        int counter = 0, end = strlen(buffer),
            incr = 0, number = 0, numToken = 0;

        if (buffer[0] == '\0') return(-1);

        while ( counter < end )
            {
            while (isspace(buffer[counter])
                    || iscntrl(buffer[counter])
                    || buffer[counter] < 0)
                counter++;
```

```
        if (isdigit(buffer[counter]))
           incr = digitstring(buffer+counter,
              p+number);

        else if (isalpha(buffer[counter]))
           incr = alphastring(buffer+counter,
              p+number);

        else if (ispunct(buffer[counter]))
           incr = punctstring(buffer+counter,
              p+number);

        if (counter < end)
           {
           pc[numToken] = p + number;
           number += incr;
           counter += --incr;
           numToken++;
           }
        };

     return(--numToken);
   }

digitstring(buffer,p)

   char buffer[], p[];

   {
      int ctr = 0;

      while (isdigit(buffer[ctr])
          && buffer[ctr] > 0)
          {
          p[ctr] = buffer[ctr];
          ctr++;
          };

      p[ctr] ='\0';

      return(++ctr);
   }
```

```
alphastring(buffer,p)

   char buffer[], p[];

   {
      int ctr = 0;

      while (isalnum(buffer[ctr])
           && buffer[ctr] > 0)
         {
         p[ctr] = buffer[ctr];
         ctr++;
         };

      p[ctr] = '\0';

      return(++ctr);
   }

punctstring(buffer,p)

   char buffer[], p[];

   {
      p[0] = buffer[0];
      p[1] = '\0';

      return(2);
   }
```

```
/* objTypes.h file */

/* Boris Allan */


int varPointer = -1,
    constPointer = -1,
    topStack = -1;

struct varObj
    {
    char name[IDSIZE];
    char assgd;
    int varVal;
    };

struct genObj
    {
    char class;
    int item;
    };

struct constObj
    {
    int constVal;
    };

struct symbolObj
    {
    char name;
    char priority;
    int (*function)();
    };

struct valObj
    {
    char class;
    int item;
    int value;
    };
```

```
struct genObj objList[MAXBUFF];

struct varObj varList[MAXBUFF];

struct constObj constList[MAXBUFF/2];

struct symbolObj delimList[2];

struct symbolObj operList[8];

struct valObj valStack[MAXBUFF/2];

popStack()
    {
    return(valStack[topStack--].value);
    }

pushStack(pushVal)
    int pushVal;
    {
    topStack++;
    valStack[topStack].value = pushVal;
    valStack[topStack].class = 'c';
    valStack[topStack].item = 0;
    }


leftParen(){}

rightParen(){}

checkVals()
    {
    static int varItem;

    if (topStack < 1)
        {
        printf("Too few items on stack\n");
        return(-1);
        }
```

```
    if (valStack[topStack-1].class == 'v')
        {
        varItem = valStack[topStack-1].item;
        if (varList[varItem].assgd == '\0')
            {
            printf("Unassigned variable\n");
            return(-1);
            }
        else
            valStack[topStack].class = 'c';
        };

    if (valStack[topStack].class == 'v')
        {
        varItem = valStack[topStack].item;
        if (varList[varItem].assgd == '\0')
            {
            printf("Unassigned variable\n");
            return(-1);
            }
        else
            valStack[topStack].class = 'c';
        };

    return(0);
    }

equalOp()
    {
    int varItem, tempVal;

    if (topStack < 1)
        {
        printf("Too few items on stack\n");
        return(-1);
        }

    if (valStack[topStack-1].class == 'c')
        {
        printf("Assignment to constant\n");
        return(-1);
        }
```

```
    varItem = valStack[topStack].item;

    if (valStack[topStack].class == 'v'
        && varList[varItem].assgd == '\0')
        {
        printf("Unassigned variable\n");
        return(-1);
        };

    tempVal = popStack();
    valStack[topStack].class = 'c';
    valStack[topStack].value = tempVal;
    varItem = valStack[topStack].item;
    varList[varItem].varVal = tempVal;
    varList[varItem].assgd = '\1';

    return(0);
    }

plusOp()
    {
    int leftVal, rightVal;

    if (checkVals() == -1) return(-1);

    rightVal = popStack();
    leftVal = popStack();
    pushStack(leftVal + rightVal);

    return(0);
    }

minusOp()
    {
    int leftVal, rightVal;

    if (checkVals() == -1) return(-1);

    rightVal = popStack();
    leftVal = popStack();
    pushStack(leftVal - rightVal);

    return(0);
    }
```

```
multOp()
    {
    int leftVal, rightVal;

    if (checkVals() == -1) return(-1);

    rightVal = popStack();
    leftVal = popStack();
    pushStack(leftVal * rightVal);

    return(0);
    }

divOp()
    {
    int leftVal, rightVal;

    if (checkVals() == -1) return(-1);

    rightVal = popStack();
    leftVal = popStack();
    pushStack(leftVal / rightVal);

    return(0);
    }

modOp()
    {
    int leftVal, rightVal;

    if (checkVals() == -1) return(-1);

    rightVal = popStack();
    leftVal = popStack();
    pushStack(leftVal % rightVal);

    return(0);
    }
```

```
powerOp()
    {
    int result, rootVal, powerVal;

    if (checkVals() == -1) return(-1);

    powerVal = popStack();

    if (powerVal < 0)
        {
        printf("Negative power\n");
        return(-1);
        };

    rootVal = popStack();

    for (result = 1; powerVal >0; powerVal--)
        result = result*rootVal;

    pushStack(result);

    return(0);
    }

negOp()
    {
    int varItem;

    if (topStack < 0)
        {
        printf("Too few items on stack\n");
        return(-1);
        }

    switch (valStack[topStack].class)
        {
        case 'v':
            varItem = valStack[topStack].item;
            if (varList[varItem].assgd == '\0')
                {
                printf("Unassigned variable\n");
                return(-1);
                };
```

```
      case 'c':
         valStack[topStack].value
            = -valStack[topStack].value;
         valStack[topStack].class = 'c';
         return(0);
      };
   }

initialize()

   {
   delimList[0].name = '(';
   delimList[0].priority = 0;
   delimList[0].function = leftParen;

   delimList[1].name = ')';
   delimList[1].priority = 10;
   delimList[1].function = rightParen;

   operList[0].name = '=';
   operList[0].priority = 1;
   operList[0].function = equalOp;

   operList[1].name = '+';
   operList[1].priority = 2;
   operList[1].function = plusOp;

   operList[2].name = '-';
   operList[2].priority = 2;
   operList[2].function = minusOp;

   operList[3].name = '*';
   operList[3].priority = 3;
   operList[3].function = multOp;

   operList[4].name = '/';
   operList[4].priority = 3;
   operList[4].function = divOp;

   operList[5].name = '%';
   operList[5].priority = 3;
   operList[5].function = modOp;
```

```
    operList[6].name = '^';
    operList[6].priority = 4;
    operList[6].function = powerOp;

    operList[7].name = '~';
    operList[7].priority = 5;
    operList[7].function = negOp;

    varPointer = -1;
    }

makeObjects(token,numTokens)

    char *token[];
    int numTokens;

    {
    int counter = 0;

    constPointer = 0;

    for (; counter <= numTokens ; counter++)
        {
        if (isdigit(token[counter][0]))
            makeConst(token[counter], counter);
        else if (isalpha(token[counter][0]))
            makeVar(token[counter], counter);
        else
            makePunct(token[counter], counter);
        };
    }

makeConst(buffer, ctr)

    char buffer[];
    int ctr;

    {
    int conValue = atoi(buffer);

    constList[constPointer].constVal
        = conValue;

    objList[ctr].class = 'c';
    objList[ctr].item = constPointer++;
    }
```

```
makeVar(buffer, ctr)

    char buffer[];
    int ctr;

    {
    int varNum = -1, varPlace = 0;

    if (strlen(buffer) > IDSIZE - 1)
        buffer[IDSIZE - 1] = '\0';

    while (varPlace <= varPointer
            && varNum == -1)
        {
        if (strcmp(buffer,varList[varPlace].name)
                == 0)
            {
            varNum = varPlace;
            varPlace = varPointer;
            }
        varPlace++;
        };

    if (varNum == -1)
        {
        varPointer = (varNum = varPlace);
        strcpy(varList[varPointer].name, buffer);
        varList[varPointer].assgd = '\0';
        };

    objList[ctr].class = 'v';
    objList[ctr++].item = varNum;
    }

makePunct(buffer, ctr)

    char buffer[];
    int ctr;

    {
    char chval = buffer[0];
```

```
switch (chval)
   {
   case '(' :
      objList[ctr].class = 'd';
      objList[ctr++].item = 0;
      break;

   case ')' :
      objList[ctr].class = 'd';
      objList[ctr++].item = 1;
      break;

   case '=' :
      objList[ctr].class = 'o';
      objList[ctr++].item = 0;
      break;

   case '+' :
      objList[ctr].class = 'o';
      objList[ctr++].item = 1;
      break;

   case '-' :
      objList[ctr].class = 'o';
      objList[ctr++].item = 2;
      break;

   case '*' :
      objList[ctr].class = 'o';
      objList[ctr++].item = 3;
      break;

   case '/' :
      objList[ctr].class = 'o';
      objList[ctr++].item = 4;
      break;
```

```
case '%' :
   objList[ctr].class = 'o';
   objList[ctr++].item = 5;
   break;

case '^' :
   objList[ctr].class = 'o';
   objList[ctr++].item = 6;
   break;

case '~' :
   objList[ctr].class = 'o';
   objList[ctr++].item = 7;
   break;

default :
   objList[ctr].class = 'e';
   objList[ctr++].item = 0;
   break;
};
}
```

```
/* rpnConv.h file */

/* Boris Allan */


struct genObj rpnList[MAXBUFF];

rpnMake(numTokens)

    int numTokens;

    {
    char typ;
    int rpnCtr, opCtr, i, opPrec, objPrec;
    static struct genObj opStack[MAXBUFF/2];

    opStack[0].class = 'o';
    opStack[0].item = -1;

    for (rpnCtr = 0, opCtr = 0, i = 0;
         i <= numTokens; i++)
      {
      typ = objList[i].class ;

      switch (typ)
          {
          case 'e':
             printf("\nInvalid symbol ");
             printf("at item %d\n",i);
             return(-1);
             break;
```

```
case 'c':
case 'v':
   rpnList[rpnCtr].class = typ;
   rpnList[rpnCtr].item
      = objList[i].item;
   rpnCtr++;
   if (objList[i+1].class == 'c'
         || objList[i+1].class == 'v')
      {
      for (; opCtr > 0; opCtr--)
         {
         if (opStack[opCtr].class
               == 'd')
            {
            printf("\nUnmatched ");
            printf("left bracket\n");
            return(-1);
            }
         else
            {
            rpnList[rpnCtr].class = 'o';
            rpnList[rpnCtr].item
               = opStack[opCtr].item;
            rpnCtr++;
            };
         };
      };
   break;
```

```
case 'd':
   if (objList[i].item == 0)
      {
      opCtr++;
      opStack[opCtr].class = 'd';
      opStack[opCtr].item = 0;
      }
   else
      {
      while (opStack[opCtr].class
               != 'd')
         {
         if (opCtr < 1)
            {
            printf("\nUnmatched ");
            printf("right bracket\n");
            return(-1);
            };
         rpnList[rpnCtr].class
            = opStack[opCtr].class;
         rpnList[rpnCtr].item
            = opStack[opCtr].item;
         opCtr--;
         rpnCtr++;
         };
      opCtr--;
      };
      break;
```

```
    case 'o':
       opCtr++;
       for (objPrec =
                   operList[objList[i].item].
                      priority;
                opPrec =
                  operList[opStack[opCtr-1].
                      item].priority,
                objPrec < opPrec
                   && opCtr > 0;
                opCtr--, rpnCtr++)
            {
            rpnList[rpnCtr].class = 'o';
            rpnList[rpnCtr].item
               = opStack[opCtr-1].item;
            };
         opStack[opCtr].class = 'o';
         opStack[opCtr].item
            = objList[i].item;
         break;
      };
   };

for (; opCtr > 0; opCtr--)
   {
   if (opStack[opCtr].class == 'd')
      {
      printf("\nUnmatched left bracket\n");
      return(-1);
      }
   else
      {
      rpnList[rpnCtr].class = 'o';
      rpnList[rpnCtr].item
         = opStack[opCtr].item;
      rpnCtr++;
      };
   };
rpnCtr--;
return(rpnCtr);
}
```

```
/* exec.h file */

/* Boris Allan */


execRpn(numTokens)

    int numTokens;
    {
    static int ctr;
    ctr = 0;
    topStack = -1;

    while (ctr <= numTokens)
        {
        switch (rpnList[ctr].class)
            {
            case 'c':
                topStack++;
                valStack[topStack].class = 'c';
                valStack[topStack].item = 0;
                valStack[topStack].value
                    = constList[rpnList[ctr].item].
                        constVal;
                break;

            case 'v':
                topStack++;
                valStack[topStack].class = 'v';
                valStack[topStack].item
                    = rpnList[ctr].item;
                valStack[topStack].value
                    = varList[rpnList[ctr].item].
                        varVal;
                break;

            case 'o':
                if (activate(operList[rpnList[ctr].
                        item].function) == -1)
                    return(-1);
                break;
            };
        ctr++;
        };
    return(topStack);
    }
```

```
activate(funcPtr)

    int (*funcPtr)();
    {
    return((*funcPtr)());
    }
```

Index